CONSIDER THE FOLLOWING

Writing from a Non-Native Perspective
Simplified with Grammar

Lectures by: Sabri g. Bebawi, Ph.D.

California, U.S.A.
Sydney, Australia

Copyright © Sabri Bebawi 2010, 2011: California, USA
All Rights Reserved

ISBN-13: 978-0615467870
ISBN-10: 0615467873

Published in the United States of America

To Khalil Gibran

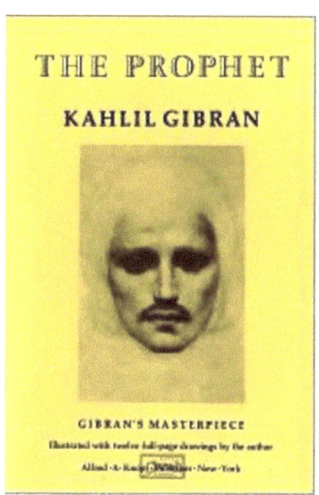

To my best friend and Muse, Lama
To Christian, Adnan, Daniel, and Nardeen

You are the rock upon which I subsist

CONTENT

1- All about Writing
2- The Function of Writing
3- Beginning to Write
4- Grammar and Writing
5- Writing Academic Essays
6- Writing Considerations
7- The Importance of Grammar
8- The Type of Essay Questions
9- The Most Important Types of Essays
10- The Non-Native Speaker

Consider the Following

Writing from a Non-Native Perspective

Simplified with Grammar

Introduction

This textbook is a writing course, which will take you from the basic idea of writing, to writing paragraphs, then to writing effective essays. The course is designed with the non-native speaker in mind, thus the content will be valuable to ESL/EFL learners as well as native speakers and any working adult.

You will learn *the basic elements of writing and the various forms of essays*. You will also enhance your revision and editing techniques, and enrich your critical-thinking and analytical skills. In doing so, you will acquire a grammar review. The materials in the course will help you develop and refine your communication and writing skills. You will learn what the process is to generate ideas, focus and narrowing your thoughts, and how to go about from the prewriting stage into a complete essay. The textbook will address the various writing modes and the organization for each mode; that is in addition to focusing on grammar, syntax, and mechanics in order to produce effective written communication

Undoubtedly, these skills will prove crucial for you, your education, and your career. One will always need to write something, whether it is a letter, a memo, a college paper, or a business document. In essence, these skills are of utmost value.

In addition, these lectures on writing, address some important practical writing concepts on which one should have command. Whether a college student or an adult in the workplace, here is what you ought to know: What prewriting, which includes brainstorming, clustering, and outlining, is. What a topic sentence is and what its characteristics are. What a thesis statement is and what makes it effective or ineffective. And what we mean when we talk about coherence, support, unity, organization and logic. Finally, and most importantly, what editing, revision, and final draft writing entail.

I hope you will find this learning experience both valuable and enriching. I also hope that you will be able to apply your new or enhanced knowledge immediately and effectively. In stating that, I mean in both verbal and written communication, as your new acquired confidence will allow you confront any language situation.

I like to end this introduction with one of my favorite quotes; it is one by Ernest Hemingway in which he cleverly and passionately states:

"All my life I've looked at words as though I were seeing them for the first time."

Ernest Hemingway

Chapter One: All about Writing

Do you think that there is a difference between writing and speaking? Most of my students' responses are "yes." Many students, in fact not only students, but most people, believe that the only difference is that writing is or should be more formal than speaking. This response may be half the truth but not the whole truth.

Body language plays a significant role in conveying what one means by the spoken message; one can immediately tell whether the speaker is happy, sad, angry, or whatever state of mind in which the speaker is. In spoken communication, we are able to explain ourselves, clarify our meaning, repeat what we say and do so many different things to get the message across. Additionally, we are able to see the listener's reaction to our message and whether the listener is paying attention and understanding the content of the message. Furthermore, if the listener is having trouble understanding our communication and requires clarification, we can always provide such clarification immediately.

Unfortunately for those of us who avoid writing and/or are scared of it, these advantages we enjoy in spoken language do not exist in writing; hence, something has to be done differently. A reader cannot call an author to ask for clarification or elaboration. This puts a writer in a rather awkward position; a writer has one chance only to get the message across; the writer may succeed or fail, but can never go back and restructure, correct, explain, or elaborate on the already written message. Perhaps that is why many of us are terrified of writing.

Consequently, if a writer wants to communicate with others effectively through writing, she/he must support any assertions made with details and solid explanation. Do not allow this to discourage you, though. The materials in this textbook will provide you with the skills you need to have good command of what is considered *Standard English*.

CONSIDER THE FOLLOWING

Get ready and have fun with this "*Standard English*." I did many, many years ago while in England learning the English language as a third language.

Standard English

Standard written English has a great value for students as well as adults in the workplace. Developing competence in speaking and writing Standard English will, without a doubt, ensure success in whatever one does since effective communication is a key to almost everything we do.

The aptitude to process and manage easily the language we use in everyday affairs will help one attain a certain power.

With "Globalization," the English language has managed to be the world's language of practically all fields: from politics, to science, to business, to literature, and even to the simplest tasks as writing a formal letter to a corporation.

So, it has become a worldwide phenomenon that more people need to learn to write English for work or school, or even personal matters. And although speaking proper English is of major significance, writing effectively and in Standard English is, perhaps, the most significant of all language skills, And that is why students have to take and pass English 100 (or some call it 101) which is a writing class, in order to be able to proceed with their educational goals.

A Glimpse at Writing Difficulties

Famous writers always remind us that no one is born a writer. All writers have to practice, practice, and practice. It is much like playing a musical instrument; one can never be proficient at it without both dedication and training. Now, that is one of the difficulties we all face when it comes to writing effectively.

Hence comes another aspect of difficulty and that is writing is not a natural activity as speaking is. Remember, no one is born a writer. It is even worse for a non-native of a language she/he is learning; it is unquestionably unnatural. I went through it. I assure you it comes with desire to learn, preparation, work, and repetition. And to put your mind at ease, there is a very simple trick to it that you will learn in this course.

Another difficulty, may be, is, as I mentioned above, that a writer has one chance only to get a message across; thus the message has to be well-defined, unambiguous, precise, and, as most of us hope, the message has to be flawless and unspoiled.

With that, another struggle is created and that is once we write and send a message, we cannot change it; we cannot correct it; and, most significantly, we cannot clarify misunderstandings or misinterpretations. This of course, makes writing an alarming experience for many because of the precision, the logic and the focus, writing demands. Although this is not easy, with patience, endurance and practice you can—and you will—accomplish it. You will write effectively.

When I think of writing while writing, I often remember the great writer Joseph Conrad, a non-native speaker. He once wrote:

"My task, which I am trying to achieve is, by the power of the written word, to make you hear, to make you feel—it is, before all, to make you see."

Writer Joseph Conrad

ESL/EFL Environment

English as a second or foreign language-writing students often have difficulties with grammatical concepts as well as with syntax (sentence structure and how the various parts of sentences go together). This, of course, may influence the quality of their writing. For this reason, acquiring grammar skills and understanding why grammatical rules the way they are become of high importance. We should admit, though, that these difficulties are not ESL/EFL learners only; they can be for native speakers, as well. This makes it necessary to review your grammar and try to understand why we structure sentences the way we do in English.

Whilst I in England learning English as a third language, I found that attaining English was neither easy nor impossible. I learned that there was always some method to grasp the rules of the English language. I had to discover and choose the best trail to follow. For me, I had to change my whole studying habits I had learned in Egypt, my native country.

For example, as children, in Egypt, we learned by memorization. However, very soon I realized that one couldn't possibly memorize a whole new language. Hence, I started learning how to reason, and tried to comprehend the rules rather than memorizing them. Once one understand a rule, one can apply it to any situation, and in language learning this is not different.

I hope my readers and my students do the same and notice that learning a new language requires time and dedication; and learning to write effectively needs a lot of practice and understanding the trick I mentioned above, I also hope that my readers and students know that their writing skills will surely improve and expand over time.

CONSIDER THE FOLLOWING 15

Learning to Write Better

I think you are probably asking yourself now "So, what one must do to become an effective writer?" There are many answers to such question since writing itself is a process. Nevertheless, there are some ways that may help you develop a better sense of advancement, as well as help you ascertain new methods and styles in your writing.

It might be an excellent idea to keep a daily journal in order to practice writing. Commenting on writing, *the great Maya Angelou* wrote: *"**There is no greater agony than bearing an untold story inside you.**"* I have kept a journal most of my life. The two books I published, *Let Me Tell You a Little Story* and *Search for Identity*, included a collection of journal entries I had written over many years.

Also, in order to boost and improve your writing skill, you ought to practice reading. Read a lot and as much as you possibly can. Pay attention to how writers express their thoughts; this way, you will not only acquire new vocabulary that will help you improve your word choice, but you will also learn about the different styles of writing and the methods writers use to organize their ideas from the start to the finish.

Again, on reading, the great Maya Angelou wrote:

"*Any book that helps a child to form a habit of reading, to make reading one of his deep and continuing needs, is good for him.*"

The Legend Maya Angelou

CONSIDER THE FOLLOWING

Keeping a portfolio of all your writings over time will be also helpful. It will help you see the growth of your writing ability and will show you your improvement, which in turn, will enhance your confidence.

Of course, these ideas do not apply to ESL/EFL only, but to all new writers, students or working adults. Now let us begin with the learning process and get on our way to become better writers.

Chapter Two: The Function of Writing

Why do we write? Think for a moment or two about that question. You will surely recognize that we write to be read; we write to others who are not materially near before us to share our thoughts with them. This is why we have to guarantee that our reader, who is not present and perhaps unknown to us, will fully comprehend what we have written without requiring further details or more information. This is why, as writers, we have to make an effort to accomplish our purpose.

Now I believe you began to develop an understanding of why writing is a problematic task for most of us, even for the best of writers. We also realize that writing is a solitary pursuit and that makes it a unique task since we receive no instant reaction or feedback or advice or reply or anything instantaneous.

Sitting at your desk writing a letter, a memo, an essay, or a term paper. You will need to ensure that your thoughts are organized and clarified in a way that your reader will have no difficulty trying to make sense of what she/he is reading.

Hence, writing is hard, yes, but it is likely to master it through instruction, repetition, drilling, and practice. But even with training and practice, there ought be a reason for writing. You must establish the reason why you are producing the piece you re writing.

Most of us write for various reasons. Here you will see some of the reasons why we labor to write something:

 We write to express ourselves:

We write our feelings and happenings in a diary, journal, or even a short poem. We do this for our personal enrichment and satisfaction.

I, for example, keep a diary. Every evening, I sit at my desk and write my moods and reactions to the happenings of the day. This certainly improves writing skills; you might want to try it.

✦ We write to provide information:

Sometimes we write to offer what we know or to help educate others about something we believe or of which we have confident knowledge. In this mode of writing, we may explain to our readers how something works, how to process something, or why a certain problem occurs.

✦ We write to persuade our readers:

Writing to persuade is, perhaps, the most difficult and critical since our main goal in writing is to motivate, to inspire, or to sway our readers and convince them through reasoning. Here we have to implement sound reasoning and solid evidence for the readers to understand and believe in what we are saying. We will focus and expand on this type of writing under "Argumentation Essays" in this textbook.

✦ We write to entertain our readers, or sometimes viewers:

The main purpose of this type of writing is to amuse. In writing this type, you will need to use humor, romance, or suspense. We encounter this type of writing every day whether in short stories, any work of fiction, or even on television and in cinema as in set comedies and films. Though this latter part, television and cinema, requires a different form of writing called screenplays, yet, it has the same idea of amusing and entertaining.

Writer Truman Capote

"To me, the greatest pleasure of writing is not what it's about, but the inner music that words make."

Chapter Three: Beginning to Write

If you have ever found yourself sitting at a desk or a table staring at a blank page trying to script a word or two and cannot, you are not alone. All of us, even the best of writers, experience and go through the same thing. Only very few experienced and famous writers, if any, can actually produce an effective piece of writing at first trial. Most of us have to think deeply, rethink deeper and rethink again before writing anything. Not only that, but we have to rewrite, revise, edit, rewrite again, and again.

At this point, I want to bring to my reader's attention that this textbook, though can be valuable for any writing environment: personal, school, or work, it focuses on the five-paragraph essay format, which is more of an academic type of essay writing and is what most schools and tests require. This format is the most introductory and multipurpose form of writing. Any standardized writing test requires that you write an essay mostly of about five paragraphs that will include an introductory paragraph, a body of at least three paragraphs, and a concluding paragraph. The same format will apply to any writings such as e-mails, memos, letters, or reports.

Here is an example. You are in school, and your teacher asks you to write an essay on the following essay topic:

> *An eventful day is one in which many unusual things take place. Think of a day in your life that was eventful and full of surprises.*

This would be a *narrative* **essay**, in which you narrate important events that have a somewhat significant impact on your life. This type of essay requires the expansion on and recounting of an incident or incidents from the moment it began to the second it ended.

So where and how do we begin? Well! Inherently, the process of writing any form of writing takes five steps.

The Writing Process

1. Prewriting
2. Outlining
3. Writing
4. Revising
5. Editing

Let us look at each process in some detail.

 Prewriting

The first stage is the creation process in which we come up with ideas and evaluate and reevaluate these concepts we create and generate. This stage of writing we refer to as part of the "prewriting" stage, which basically includes ***Brainstorming, Clustering***, and ***Outlining***; in all, it is really devising. While brainstorming, we have to jot down our thoughts on paper without worrying about grammar or syntax, or even spelling. We need to be free of all the chains of rules in order to create. If you have a writing task, try to ask questions and answer them. In doing so, you will be able to generate an innovative and inventive vision about which you will write.

This is the first step in the writing process. Here you try to create ideas for discussion and writing; then you attempt to focus and narrow the ideas you have for the points you want to make. You achieve this through *brainstorming*, *clustering*, and any other means to focus your thoughts around your purpose for writing.

First, you will need to ***brainstorm***. Using the essay topic above, think of a day that you will always remember, and list the reasons why you will always remember that day. Write a list of as many events that took place on that day as you can.

 Clustering

Second, you will need to *cluster* and narrow down these events to the most intriguing and interesting three events. Write down the events and the reasons why they are interesting.

So, let us assume, for example, you want to write that essay on the most eventful day in your life that I mentioned above. So you *brainstorm* and you try to generate ideas; certainly, you have many eventful days in your life, but you want to select a day that is most memorable and that would interest your readers. You also need a day that had many unusual events. Once you have thought of several days one of which you can write about, then list these days in what we call *Clustering* technique. This clustering techniques helps you narrow down the ideas you have generated and focus on one topic about which you will write.

Writers often do this in the following way:

The day I had my 21st birthday	The day I went to New York
The first day at my new college	The day my doctor told me bad news

CONSIDER THE FOLLOWING

Now, you have managed to think of three significant days in your life and written them down in the above cluster. The next step is to expand on that by thinking of what the significant events were that made that particular day eventful or memorable.

In the graph below, list the days above in the first four boxes, then narrow them down in the two boxes, finally decide on the day you think you can write a lot about and you think your readers will find interesting to read.

CONSIDER THE FOLLOWING

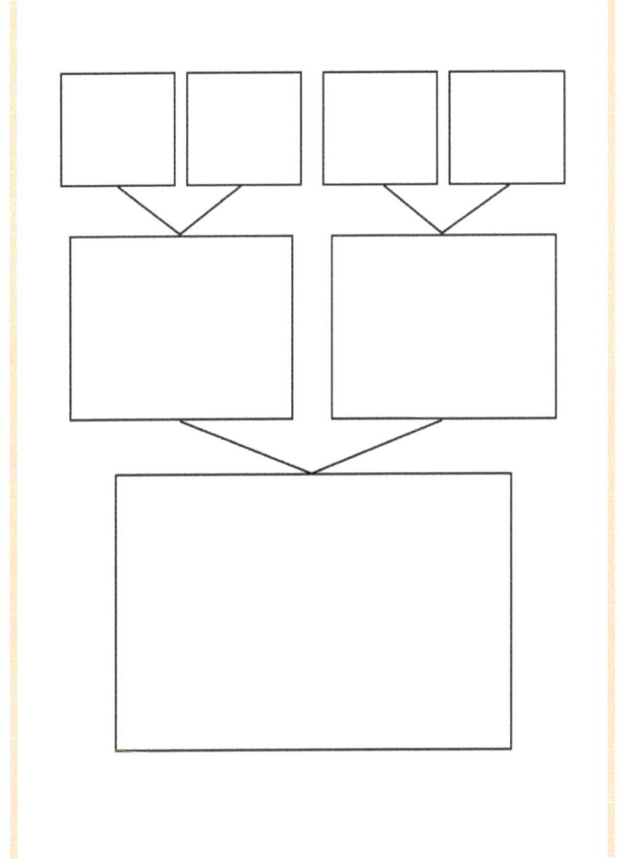

Brain Storming and Clustering Stage

CONSIDER THE FOLLOWING

By now you have completed part of the first stage, ***prewriting.*** You have taken care of the **brainstorming** and the **clustering** and now you know your choice and what your essay will address. Here comes the last part of prewriting, which is the ***outlining***.

♦ Outlining

From your cluster, you will decide on where your essay is going and what the focus will be. Here comes the organization of your ideas and you do this in an outline format so that you can refer to it all the time as you proceed with writing your essay. So, it is a logical, general description of what you will write. It is a summary and a visual design of your writing.

Your outline will reflect your logical thinking and your clear classification. **A badly organized outline will certainly reflect on the final product of writing**. Organization is of utmost importance, and it is not that difficult to master. You will soon find that the outline helps you organize your ideas and present your material in a connected form.

Your outline will guide you through the actual writing of the essay. Here is how it should look like. If you keep this picture in your mind all the time, you will find writing to be much easier than you had ever thought.

Again, please keep the picture of the following outline format in your thoughts and all you will need to do is fill in the information you gathered through the previous brainstorming stages. Also, it is encouraging to know that this applies to all forms of writings even it were a 50-page term paper; the same concept of outlining applies.

I. **Introduction**
   - The Topic
   - The Thesis (or the main idea)

II. **First Idea**
   - Idea
   - Details

III. **Second Idea**
   - Idea
   - Details

IV. **Third Idea**
   - Idea
   - Details

V. **Conclusion**
   - Restating the Thesis Statement
   - Writing an Afterthought

Sample outline for writing an essay

CONSIDER THE FOLLOWING   29

Well done! Now, merely, for the five-paragraph essay, you will need to write a well-organized and attention-getter introductory paragraph in which you will use two or three sentences to introduce your topic. Your introductory paragraph will include what we call a *Thesis Statement*, which you will learn about a little later in the book. But for now, you need to know that the thesis statement is the main idea of the essay – it is what the whole essay will be about.

After your introductory paragraph, you will go on to the body which, again in the five-paragraph essay, consists of three paragraphs and each paragraph must have what we call a **Topic Sentence**, which is the controlling idea of the paragraph. You will learn more about the topic sentence also later in the book. After this is done, you will write a conclusion that wraps up all the information in the essay.

Now you are on your way to writing your essay.

✢ Writing

In this stage of the writing process, a writer pays close attention to the reason or purpose of the work. Once this purpose is clear, writing the first draft begins. This first draft is the materialization of the ideas developed in the previous writing stages.

You must follow the outline before starting to write your essay. And before you begin, you need to develop a strong ***thesis statement***, which is basically the sentence that shows what your ideas to be developed are. Once you created this thesis statement, then begin writing your introductory paragraph. The introductory paragraph will include a sentence or two to introduce your topic followed by the thesis statement you have developed.

Here is an example of an introductory paragraph on the essay "An eventful day in your life" written by one of my students:

> *"The most important day I remember in all of my life is the day when there was a public memorial for Michael Jackson. It was also the day when I found out I would never be able to bare children. It was on July 7th, 2009 when my world was forever changed, and how I saw things around me would never be the same. This was the day that I lost my faith in God."*

The student introduced the topic in the first two sentences, and then moved to state the thesis statement with the following ideas:

- The world was forever changed;
- How the writer saw things would never be the same; and
- The writer lost faith in God.

From here, the student continued to develop each of these three ideas in one paragraph adding supporting details as examples and descriptions of the events and the effects.

As for you, once you have written your introductory paragraph, you will now develop your ideas in the body of the essay, giving as many supporting examples as you can to make your essay interesting.to read.

Ernest Hemingway in Paris

The process does not stop here. Once an essay is completed, we need to take another look at it to ensure what we wrote is what we actually wanted to say. Here comes the next stage we call *revision*.

✤ Revising

In this stage, you will present an ultimate structure to your piece of writing. Also, in this stage we often ensure that our voice or declaration is consistent and unswerving. It could be serious, intellectual, or funny. All what you have written in the first draft needs to be polished, refined and –as much as possible- perfected.

All irrelevant materials should be deleted and all illogical conclusions should be revised. You need to ensure that each single point you have written does not stray or drift from your main focus.

At times, you will discover that you need to add more supporting details to get your ideas across smoothly. There are other issues we will learn as we progress with our reading of this textbook. Next comes each writer's haunting task, including me, and that is the editing stage. Though most professional writers have editors who edit their work for them, we do not have such luxury; we have to edit our work ourselves, and sometimes that is not an easy task.

Editing

In the editing stage, you need to check not only for spelling and grammar errors, but also for the effectiveness of the transitions between ideas in each paragraph and between paragraphs themselves. Transitions can be words or phrases, and they are imperative because they connect your essay and make it coherent and flow easily, showing the linkage between a notion and the thought that follows it.

If, for example, you want to indicate an addition, you would use words such as:

- In addition
- Furthermore
- Moreover
- Also
- Equally important

If you want to exhibit a contrast, you would use words such as:

- However
- On the other hand
- Although
- But

If you require concluding, you would use words like:

- Therefore
- Thus
- In conclusion

CONSIDER THE FOLLOWING 33

You generally put a transitional word or phrase at the beginning of the paragraph to connect it to the one before it. One very valuable way to generate a transition sentence is to identify a key word or phrase in the previous sentence and repeat it in your transition sentence.

In this correcting stage, you will also need to check for the elaboration of any generalized ideas and the supporting evidence, such as details, illustrations, and examples. You must check your sentence structure, re-examine the precision and intelligibility of the words you chose, and exclude fragments, run-on sentences, comma splices, and clichés. Moreover, check for such grammatical mistakes as inconsistent verb tenses, subject-verb disagreement, and plural and singular noun shifts. All these terms might sound scary, but worry not for we shall learn about them soon in the following chapters.

Now your paper is ready for your readers to read.

Chapter Four: Grammar and Writing

Let us think together. What is that thing called grammar anyway?

Well, do you have a pet? If you do, do you observe carefully what your pet does sometimes?

Watching animals can be a charming involvement. You perhaps wonder sometimes if your pet thinks and tries to communicate with you.

The feeling is most probably your pet does think and tries to communicate with you. You are not far off. If so, then what is the difference between your pet's communication and that of ours as persons? Well, the difference is that thing called ***Grammar***. Your pet might be able to communicate but your pet cannot tell of the past or explain events that will happen. Your pet communicates *in the now*, the present. We, on the other hand, can tell stories of the past and talk of the future. **Grammar allows us the luxury of displacement of time and space.** Chatting with one another, we take our concepts to different times and distinct places.

Let us take a close look at the following account of events:

> *Last summer I went to Rome and Barcelona to see my family. I had a magnificent time. In Barcelona, I saw much art and very interesting buildings. In Rome, I went to the to the house where I had lived before I came to the United States. In both places, I appreciated my time with my family.*

In the short paragraph above, I caught you to go with me to a separate time (last summer) and to two different places.

And that is ***grammar***. Only the human animal can do that (except for bees that can tell other bees where food is and how far it is). We can take our thoughts to different times and different places. This form of time and space displacement is ***that thing we call grammar***. So, grammar is the way we use language to express ideas that tell about different places and different times. For us to interconnect unmistakably, we must use grammar effectively.

For example, what is wrong with this picture?

"I went to a party tomorrow"? Well! What do you think?

I used a verb in the past (went) while referring to the future (tomorrow) so the time displacement is erroneous, isn't it?

And this is grammar. Grammar is to express our thoughts about things that happen in different times and different places. Animals cannot do that, at least as far as we know now; we can. Lucky for us, isn't it?

When we talk of grammar, in general terms, we are referring to the time when an action takes, took, or will take place. Everything we talk about is in the present, the past, or the future. We have a set system to indicate these times. This is what we will examine here.

I hope you will enjoy this as much as I anticipate. I learned English as a foreign language and went through what you, if you are a non-native speaker, are going through now; I think, perhaps, my own experiences with learning languages will help me show you some feasible ways to learn English.

Like any language, English verb tenses (times) are the future, the present and the past. Each of these times can be specified in terms of simple, continuous (some books and teachers refer to it as progressive), perfect and perfect continuous (progressive). Let us identify each of theses time references.

The Simple Tense

The present simple indicates that the act happens habitually. We use time words that show that. Some of these words are: ***always, often, seldom, sometimes, rarely, never, usually, and frequently***.

Example: *I rarely visit theaters.*

Past simple means that the act took place once in the past. Time words that will show such meaning may include: ***yesterday, last night, last week, last year*** and any other word that indicate past.

Example: *I studied at the library last night.*

Future simple means that the act will happen once in the future. Time words that indicate such tense may include, ***tomorrow, next week, next year, and later*** and any other word that will show future.

Example: *I will visit you tomorrow.*

The problem is that it does not end here. We have other issue to tackle, and that is verb forms.

Verb Forms

Verb forms are modified to specify the time in which the act occurs. In the present, verbs do not change unless the subject is a singular third party: ***he, she and it***.

To explain this, let us look at verb to study. In the present time we will say:

> *I study every day.*

> *You study everyday.*

CONSIDER THE FOLLOWING

We study everyday.

They study everyday.

Notice that action *work* has not been altered. It stays in the same form. However, watch what happens here:

*She stud**ies** everyday.*

*He stud**ies** everyday.*

*It stud**ies***, if you can say such a thing, everyday.

Notice that the actions are terminated with in **(s)** to suggest singular third party **he, she and it.**

♦ The Past Tense

In the past, the action form changes to reveal the past. Most verbs in English end in (-ed) when used in the past.

Let us consider the verb 'play' in the past:

- I play**ed** yesterday.
- You play**ed** yesterday.
- We play**ed** yesterday.
- They play**ed** yesterday.
- She play**ed** yesterday.
- He played yesterday.
- It played yesterday.

Notice that the verb ends in (-ed) every time notwithstanding of the subject of the sentence.

In English, however, like many languages, we have many verbs that are irregular and take different forms. Their forms change. Do you know why? Well! Neither do I. A good example of these verbs is 'to write' which in the past changes to 'wrote'.

*I **wrote** a letter to my family **yesterday***.

It might be a good idea to try to watch for such verbs as you are studying.

The future is the simplest. All we do is adding **will** before the verb.

For example: I **will go** to school tomorrow.

 Three Major Verbs in English

When I was learning English as a third language, I found that there are three very unusual, yet very important verbs. These verbs are unusual in their usage as well as in their meaning. Similar to some languages, and unlike many others, English verbs *to be, to do* and *to have* are very peculiar. They are used on one hand as main verbs with their own meaning,

For example:

- I am a student.
- I do my homework everyday.
- I have a car.

On the other hand, they function as helping verbs without a meaning of their own but they add to the meaning of the verb they are helping, for example:

- I am studying.
- What did you say?
- I have done my homework.

Let me try to clarify the meaning and usage of these verbs.

 **The Verb *'To Be'***

Similarly to most languages on this planet, the verb *'to be'* is the backbone of the linguistic structure of English. It does not indicate an action. It describes a state of being; it is a verb of existence. It is what I am, what you are or what one is – not what one does, but what one is. However, this verb may be used to assist other verbs in creating a special tense (time) or a special structure. In order for one to be able to manipulate this verb, one must learn to conjugate it with the various nouns and/or pronouns.

The following is a list of the most possible forms the verb to be may appear in:

Present Simple	Past Simple	Future Simple
I am a student.	I was a student.	I will be at school tomorrow.
You are a student.	You were a student.	You will be at school tomorrow.
We are students.	We were students.	We will be at school tomorrow.
They are students.	They were students.	They will be at school tomorrow.
He is a student.	He was a student.	He will be at school tomorrow.
She is a student.	She was a student.	She will be at school tomorrow.
It is a car.	It was sunny yesterday.	It will be sunny tomorrow.

CONSIDER THE FOLLOWING

Present Progressive	Past Progressive	Future Progressive
I am being	I was being	It is awkward to use, thus never used- however, just to know the rule, you add will for the future.
You are being	You were being	
They are being	We were being	
He is being	They were being	
She is being	He was being	
Pay attention to this form; it is most confusing to learners of English.	She was being	
	It was being	

CONSIDER THE FOLLOWING

Present Perfect	Past Perfect	Future Perfect
I have been a student for one year.	I had been	I will have been
You have been a student for one year.	You had been	You will have been
We have been students for one year.	We had been	We will have been
They have been students for one year.	They had been	They will have been
He has been a student for one year.	He had been	He will have been
She has been a student for one year.	She had been	She will have been
It has been sunny all week.	It had been	It will have been.

CONSIDER THE FOLLOWING

 The Verb *'To Have'*

To ESL/EFL language learners, the verb *to have* may cause some confusion. It is, without a doubt, an unfamiliar verb in the sense that it functions in various ways, which can be puzzling. However, if the learner can identify the three different ways this verb is used, he or she will find that the formula is rather simple.

(1) ***"To Have"* as a main verb**

The verb *to have* functions as any other action verb and it implies the meaning of possession.

For example, when one says: "*I have a car*," "*I have a house*," or "*I have a book*," one means that she or he possesses a car, a house, or a book.

I have	*You have*	*She has*	*He has*
We have	*They have*	*It has*	

(Notice that the third party singular takes *s*-has.)

I had	*You had*	*She had*	*He had*
We had	*They had*	*It had*	

(Notice that all nouns and pronouns take "had " in the past tense.)

I am having	*You are having*	*She is having*	*He is having*
We are having	*They are having*	*It is having*	

CONSIDER THE FOLLOWING

(Notice the use of the verb *to be* + have + -ing; this is the present progressive tense. To make the past progressive tense, you just change the verb to be to the past.)

I have had   *You have had*   *She has had*

We have had   *They have had*   *It has had*

(Notice the use of the verb *to have* twice. Although this may confuse you, you should realize that the first time to have is used as an auxiliary, and the second time is the actual verb meaning to own. Notice that has is used with she/he/it; this is particularly confusing to ESL/EFL students. It will be explained when we discuss the perfect tense.)

(2) *"To Have"* as a Helping Verb

The verb *to have* is also used as an auxiliary to help other verbs create the perfect tense, for example,

- *I have studied English for five years.*
- *I have visited Vietnam.*

This does not pose a problem except when the main verb is the verb to have meaning to own or possess.

For example,

- *I have had my car for ten years.*

Have here is the auxiliary and had is the main verb in the *–en* form.

Therefore, you ought to remember that verb *to have* functions both as a main verb meaning to own and as an auxiliary verb to help other verbs create the perfect tense.

CONSIDER THE FOLLOWING

(3) **The Use of "*Have To*"**

In addition to the two forms you learned above, there is another use for have in the expression have to; meaning must. This, of course, must be followed by another verb.

For example,

I have to visit my brother tonight.

She has to see the doctor.

And in the past tense,

We had to write a paragraph.

The Verb '*To Do*'

To do is also an unfamiliar verb and can be baffling to non-native English speakers. Because of the lack of exact translation of the verb *to do* in other languages, non-native speakers confuse it with the verb **to make**. In fact, most French and Spanish dictionaries list the verb *to do* as the verb *to make*. This, however, is not essentially true. While verb *to do* and *to make* may intersect in other languages, in English they are two separate verbs, distinguished and with different meanings. Hence, to fully understand this verb, one must look at it with only an English eye; this means that one must not try to translate this action verb literally.

Verb *to do* functions as a main verb with its own meaning that is very different from make. For example,

- I do my homework every day.
- I do my laundry every Saturday, but
- I make coffee every morning
- I make dinner every night.

CONSIDER THE FOLLOWING

More Functions for Verb "*To Do*"

While verb *to do* works as a main verb, it also functions in two separate ways: as an emphasis verb and as an auxiliary verb in the question form.

(1) For Emphasis

***To do* may be used to emphasize another verb, to put stress on it, or to make it stand out.** This is used more in British English than American.

Example, when one says:

- "Do come in."
- "Do sit down."
- "Do call at any time."

(2) For questions and negative statements

Verb *to do* is also used as an auxiliary verb that helps create questions. For example, one must ask, did you go to school yesterday? And not, "You went to school yesterday?" All questions about actions must include verb *to do* unless the question is a perfect tense in a progressive form.

To do is used to make action verbs negative, as in, "I don't get up early," or "Bill didn't come to class," unless the negative statement is in a perfect or progressive tense.

Tenses and Forms of Verbs

The following may help you avoid errors in verb tenses or verb forms:

Just like most languages, English verbs have several forms, and each verb tense uses a particular form. These are the possible forms followed by two examples, a regular verb and an irregular verb:

CONSIDER THE FOLLOWING

Infinitive: To work – to eat
Simple: work (s)- eat (s)
Progressive: working – eating
Past: worked – ate
Past participle: worked – eaten

Note: Some books refer to the progressive form as the present participle and to the past participle as the *–en* form. Also, the term *continuous* is sometimes used instead of *progressive*.

Verb tenses are divided into three major times:

Future   *Present*   *Past*

Each time is divided into four different tenses:

Simple   *Progressive*   *Perfect*   *Perfect Progressive*

To review once more, we looked at all possible verb tenses and forms and we decided that English verbs have several forms, and each verb tense uses a particular form. Here we will look at these tenses and forms and try to make sense out of them. We will examine when and how we use each form.

These are the possible forms followed by two examples, a regular verb and an irregular verb:

- Infinitive: To work- to eat
- Simple: work (s)- eat (s)
- Progressive: working – eating
- Past: worked – ate
- Past participle: worked – eaten

Verb tenses are divided into three major times:

CONSIDER THE FOLLOWING

- The future
- The present
- The past

Each of these times has four different specific times:

- The simple
- The progressive
- The perfect
- The perfect progressive

We have looked at the simple and the progressive. Here, we will examine the perfect tense in the present and past times. We will look at when, how, and why the perfect tense is used.

Again, remember that verb tenses reflect important information about the time of the action. To illustrate, let us examine the following chart:

CONSIDER THE FOLLOWING

TIME	ACTION
6:30 a.m.	Get up
7:00 a.m.	Make breakfast
7:45 a.m.	Go to school
9:00 a.m.	Attend English class
12:15 p.m.	Talk with Mary
12:30 p.m.	Eat lunch
3:30 p.m.	Study at the library
4:30 p.m.	Go to work

Now let us ask some questions about the activities in the chart.

The Present Simple Tense:

Q. What does Sabri do every day at 7:00?
A. Sabri *makes* breakfast *every day* at 7:00.

The Present Progressive Tense:

Q. It is 9:00 now. What is Sabri doing now?
A. Sabri *is attending* English class *now.*

The Past Simple Tense:

Q. What did Sabri do yesterday?
A. Sabri *got up* at 6:30, *made* breakfast at 7:00, *went* to school at 7:45, *attended* English class at 9:00, *ate* lunch at 12:15 and *went* to work at 4:30.

The Past Progressive Tense:

Q. What was Sabri doing yesterday at 12:15?
A. Sabri *was talking* to Mary *yesterday at 12:15.*

The Future Simple Tense:

Q. What will Sabri do tomorrow at 7:45?
A. Sabri *will go* to school *tomorrow* at 7:45.

The Future Progressive Tense:

Q. What will Sabri be doing tomorrow at 2:30?
A. Sabri *will be studying* in the library *tomorrow at 2:30.*

About The Past Progressive Tense

First, we need to recognize that this is ***past***. Then, we need to realize it is ***progressive***. So these two points we have to bear in mind. So, if for example you are talking about an act you did yesterday. For example: ***I studied yesterday at the library***. If you wish to stress the continuity of the action since it took you sometime to study, then you may say: ***I was studying at the library yesterday***.

If someone asks you: ***"Where were you yesterday?"*** Your answer most certainly will be ***"I was studying at the library."***

We use the past progressive also when we speak of two actions that took place in the past, and one interrupted the other. For example: ***"While I was studying at the library yesterday, I saw Maria."*** - Here you were studying and in the middle of your study, you encountered Maria.

The Future Perfect Tense

From the chart above, on page 39, you probably now know how the perfect tense is formed. The only problematic perfect tense seems to be the future perfect.

CONSIDER THE FOLLOWING

We said that the perfect tense is formed by using ***verb have + the main verb in the past participle***. For example, ***I have eaten***. In the present perfect, helping verb *have* is in the present. In the past perfect, helping verb *have* is in the past. In the future, helping verb have is in the future. Simple. Don't you think?

So, by definition the future perfect tense is one that shows the action will be complete in the future. Let us assume that I came to the United States in 1995. Consider the following sentences:

> *I have been in the United States for five years.*

This present perfect sentence means that I came to the US 5 years ago; I am in the US now, and I will probably be in the US in the future.

> *I had been in the US for four years last December.*

This past perfect sentence means that last December I completed four years of living in the US.

> *I will have been in the United States for six years next December.*

This future perfect sentence says that I have not finalized six years in the US yet, but the six years will be whole next December, in the future.

So, the future perfect tense means that the action is not complete yet, but will be in the future. The formula ***for the future perfect is will have + verb in the past participle.***

For example:

- I will have eaten by the time you come.
- I will have learned English grammar by the end of this course.
- I will have finished this lesson in one hour.

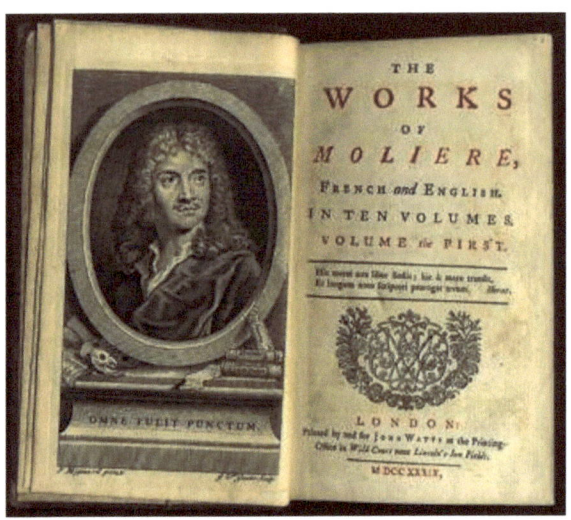

Moliere, French Dramatist

CONSIDER THE FOLLOWING

All about Modals

Making Sense of the Modals

When I was studying ESL in London, England, Modals were among the most thought-provoking ideas for me. I could not understand, for example, why we used the past form of the modal *would* in present sentences, such as "Would you bring me a cup of tea?" or "Could you help me?" It took me a while before I was able to recognize English modals and their function.

Well, I will share with you my conclusions about modals, what they really mean, how they are used, and when and under what conditions we can use them.

Clarifying the Meaning of Modals

As it was the case with me, the meaning of modals can be mystifying to an ESL learner. In traditional grammar books we often find large charts, which attempt to summarize the form and meaning of modals. Such presentations give a rather disjointed view of the modals. Here, we will give consideration to the semantic meaning in which modals are used.

Using Modals in Social Interaction:

1. One major system in the social use of modals entails making requests.

   These can be requests of a general nature:

   Will

   Would   You help me with this exercise?

   Can

CONSIDER THE FOLLOWING

    Could

1. Or can be specific requests for permission:

    May

    Might

          I go home early?

    Can

    Could

The second major system in the social interactional use of modals involves the giving of advice.

    You might take an English class.
    You could take an English class.
    You should take an English class.
    You had better take an English class.
    You must take an English class.

Notice that each sentence above reflects the authority of the speaker. Authority of the speaker or urgency of the message increases.

Logical Probability - Uses of Modals

The logical use of some of the same modals typically deals with an inference or prediction, for example:

Juan: Someone is at the door.
Martha: It may be Suzan. (Inference)

Notice now that in the following examples the degree of certainty regarding inference increases:

    Juan: Someone is knocking.

CONSIDER THE FOLLOWING

Martha: That could be Suzan

That might be Suzan.
That may be Suzan.
That should be Suzan.
That must be Suzan.

Other Uses of Modals

There are four other uses of modals that are somewhat different from the uses described above. They are:

Ability-can, be able to:

- I can speak Spanish.
- Suzan is able to run fast

Desire-would like to:

- Sarah would like to go to Paris.

Offer-would you like?

- Would you like anything to eat?

Preference-would rather, would prefer to:

- I would rather study languages than math.
- Suzan would prefer to go to school instead of working.

Additional Information on Modals

The negation of a modal (meaning to use a modal in the negative form)

To use a modal in a negative sentence, we put *not* after the modal, for example:

CONSIDER THE FOLLOWING

- I cannot do it.
- I am not able to do it
- We will not eat there.
- We are going to eat at that restaurant
- You should not smoke in here.
- You are not supposed to smoke here.

Notice that pair of sentences above shares the same meaning. However, the following is different:

- You must not go.
- You do not have to go

The meaning is clearly different. While the first is a command, the second is not. It is more of a choice.

Making Sense of It All

Now let me try to help you make sense out of this. Modals are words that express *possibility*, *authority*, *advice* or *ability*. The level of certainty and/or the level of ability control which modal to use. Let us look at this:

CONSIDER THE FOLLOWING

May	**Possibility**
Might	

Can	**Ability**
Could	

Will	**Possibility and/or ability**
Would	

Should	**Advice**

Must	**Command**

Degrees of Certainty: Future Time

We have examined the use of modals in the present and past times. Now let us examine their use in future time. Well, *should* and *ought to* can be used to express expectations about future events.

For example:

> *Maria has been studying hard.*
> *She should do well on the test tomorrow.*

Or

> *She ought to do well on the test tomorrow.*

CONSIDER THE FOLLOWING

In these two possible sentences, the speaker is saying, "Maria will probably do well on the test. I expect her to do well. That is what I think will happen."

Your textbook, *Understanding and Using English Grammar* provides a wealth of examples and many exercises that would be very helpful here.

Progressive Forms of Modals:

The progressive (or continuous as some texts call it) form of modals can be in present or past. Certainly you remember the formula for the progressive, don't you? Well, ***just to refresh your memory, it is the verb to be + the verb in the -ing form***.

So present progressive will be something like this:

➕ *I am studying grammar now.*

And past progressive:

➕ *I was studying grammar last night.*

Again, progressive is **the verb *to be* + a verb + -ing.**

So, logically, a modal in the present progressive will be something like this:

➕ *Sabri may be sleeping.*

(Modal) May (Verb To Be) Be (Verb) Sleep with **ing**.

Another example:

> "*All of the lights in Ann's room are turned off. She must be sleeping.*"

CONSIDER THE FOLLOWING

Here is a tricky situation. You remember we said that modals in the past are ***modals + perfect; example***:

> ***He must have been tired.***

Then modals in the past progressive will have to be:

Modal + perfect progressive: Modal + have + been + verb + ing

> She must have been sleeping.
> He might have been studying.
> She could have been playing.

These mean that the action in progress at a time in the past.

Well, let us recapitulate. We discussed the modals, their meaning and their various uses.

Modals are helping words that are used to express:

(1) *Possibility*

(2) *Ability*

(3) *Degree of Certainty* and

(4) *Level of authority*.

And we also stressed that:

The degree of possibility decreases as we use the past for of the modal:

I may visit you tonight. (50% chance that I will)
I might visit you tonight. (It is less than 50% chance I will)
I can run fast. (I am positively sure I can)
I could run fast. (I am not 100% sure - possibility may depend on something else)

CONSIDER THE FOLLOWING 60

Will you shut the door? (You are close to the door and the possibility of you shutting it is high)
Would you shut the door? (You are far from the door and you might not want to go shut it)
You should study harder. (I am advising you without authority)
You must study harder. (I am commanding you with authority)

Would and *Could* in the Past:

One more matter to tackle with is the use of *would* to express a repeated action in the past and the use of *could* to express ability in the past. I will try to simplify this as much as possible. Here it is:

When *would* is used in the past, it means *used to*, for example:

When I was younger, I would run two hours every day.

This means that I used to run two hours every day and now I don't.

Another example:

When I was in Paris, I would spend hours walking up and down the Champs-Elysees.

This means that I used to do that when I was in Paris.

When *could* is used in the past, it means was able to.

For example:

 My girlfriend could lift the desk, but I could not.

This means that my girlfriend was able to lift the desk, but I was unable to.

Remember that there are nine (9) main modals in English. They are:

CONSIDER THE FOLLOWING

- Shall
- Will
- Can
- May
- Must
- Should
- Would
- Could
- Might

Modals are used to help convey a specific meaning. They indicate degree of possibility, probability, authority, or ability.

Remember that *would*, *could* and *might* are used when the degree of probability is 50% less. *Should* is used to offer advice and must is used to express an order or a command; so, the degree of authority is different between the two. Also notice that *shall* is no longer used in American English except in stating a question. For example, *"Shall we go to the theater?" "Shall we call Mary?"*

We shall see grammar come back in Chapter Seven where we will discuss the importance of grammar in writing.

Clauses and Phrases

Perhaps you have encountered words like 'phrase' or 'clause' and wondered what they are and what they mean. Wonder no longer. We will also examine them and how questions are formed in English. This is particularly important because English may be a little different from other languages.

First, let us identify what is a **phrase** and what is a **clause**.

A *phrase* is a group of words that does not include a subject and a verb. In English, objects often follow verbs. The object is usually a *noun phrase*.

For example: *I know this book.*

I = subject
Know = verb
this book = noun phrase

Notice that *"this book"* is just a group of words that does not contain a subject and a verb.

A *clause* is a group of related words that has a subject and a verb. Some verbs can be followed by a noun clause.

For example: *I know where she lives*

I = subject
Know = verb
Where she lives = noun clause

Notice that *"where he lives"* is a *clause* because it contains a subject (she) and a verb (lives). Notice also that *where he lives* is the object of the verb *"know."*

CONSIDER THE FOLLOWING

Types of Clauses

There are two types of clauses: *dependen*t and *independent.*
A dependent clause is one that cannot stand alone as a sentence. It must depend on another clause that is independent. *An independent clause* is a group of related words that contains a subject and a verb and can stand alone as a complete sentence.

Questions vs. Statements:

Let us review some basics of English grammar.

For example:

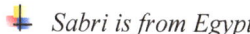 *Sabri is from Egypt.*

Sabri = subject
is = verb
From Egypt = complement (prepositional phrase because *from* is a preposition)

In English all sentences are formed in the same way, subject + verb + complement. The verb is always after the subject

Now notice the way we make questions:

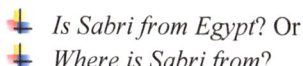 *Is Sabri from Egypt?* Or
Where is Sabri from?

Notice that the verb comes before the subject. So, in questions we place the verb before the subject. The placement of the verb before the subject is what tells us that the form is a question. *Remember that it is not the question word that forms a question; it is the position of the verb.*

CONSIDER THE FOLLOWING

 ### The Noun Clause

The following question words can be used to introduce a noun clause: *when, where, why, how, who, whom, what, which, whose.*

Example:

Answer this question using 'I don't know.'

Where does Sabri live?

I don't know _____.

It is incorrect to say, "I don't know where does he live."

Notice that *does he live* is a question form. *Noun clauses cannot be in question form*; it has to be a statement.

"*I don't know where he lives*" is the correct answer.

I hope this makes sense. Practice by asking questions and reply by starting I do not know then put the subject before the verb: *I do not know where he lives; I do not know how old she is; I do not know how fat the library is.*

 ### The Adjective Clause

An adjective clause is a dependent clause that modifies a noun. It describes, identifies, or gives further information about a noun. An adjective clause is also called a *relative clause.*

An adjective clause uses pronouns to connect the dependent clause to the independent clause. The adjective clause pronouns are who, whom, which, that, and whose. Adjective clause pronouns are also called relative pronouns.

CONSIDER THE FOLLOWING

Let us look at these sentences:

I thanked the teacher.

The teacher helped me.

We can connect these two sentences using the second as an adjective clause.

 *I thanked the teacher who helped me.*

Who helped me is an adjective clause that modifies the noun *teacher*.

Remember that the adjective clause closely follows the noun it modifies.

Study how these pairs of sentences are combined:

He is the English teacher.
I told you about him.

- He is the English teacher about whom I told you.
- He is the English teacher whom I told you about.
- He is the English teacher I told you about.

Notice that if the preposition comes at the beginning of the adjective clause, only *whom* or *which* may be used. *That* or *who* never immediately follows a preposition.

The Adverb Clause

Adverb clauses are dependent clauses. They cannot stand alone as a sentence. They must be connected to an independent clause.

Example:

CONSIDER THE FOLLOWING

- When I was in London, I saw several plays.
- I saw several plays when I was in London.

Here is a list of words used to introduce adverb clauses.

Note: They are also called *Subordinating Conjunctions*.

Words that introduce adverbs of time:

After	By the time that	The first time that	While
As	Every time that	Until	
As soon as	Once	When	
Before	Since	Whenever	

Words that introduce adverbs of cause and effect:

Because	Now that	Since

Words that introduce adverbs of contrast:

Although	Though	Whereas
Even though	While	

Words that introduce adverbs of condition:

Even if	In the event that	Whether or not
If	Only if	
In case	Unless	

CONSIDER THE FOLLOWING

Example:

> 🞣 *Because he was sick, he stayed at home.*
> 🞣 *He stayed at home because he was sick.*

Notice the punctuation in the first sentence. If the adverb clause comes at the beginning of the sentence, we must put a comma after it. This is a rule in English, and it is crucial that you remember it.

The Rule Is:

If the sentence begins with a dependent clause, we must add a comma to separate it from the independent clause.

Reducing Adjective Clauses to Phrases

Remember, we decided that:

> A clause is a group of words that has a subject and a verb.

> 🞣 *A clause can be independent, meaning that it can stand-alone as a complete thought.*
> 🞣 *A clause can also be dependent, meaning that it cannot stand alone, and it needs another thought to complete it.*
> 🞣 *Clauses can be reduced to phrases. A phrase is merely a group of words that does not have a subject or a verb.*

Example:

> ✓ *The girl who is talking to Sabri is from China.*

Who is talking to Sabri is an adjective clause. We can change it to an adjective phrase by *omitting the subject who and the verb is*.

The girl talking to Sabri is from China.

Talking to Sabri is an adjective phrase reduced from the adjective clause '*who is talking to Sabri.*'

Some adverb clauses can be confusing when you try to change them to phrases.

I hope this gives you a broader understanding of how these issues are significant while writing. I also hope that you have acquired an idea and a significant comprehension to watch for errors in these areas in your writing while writing and during the revision and the editing stages.

Chapter Five: Writing Academic Essays

I hope you recall reading in Chapter Three that this textbook focuses on the five-paragraph essay format, which is more of an academic type of essay writing and is what most schools and tests require. In order to allow more learners from various fields, whether academic or the work place, to benefit from these lectures, I elected to focus on the five-paragraph essay format.

This format is the most introductory and multipurpose form of writing. Any standardized writing test requires that you write an essay mostly of about five paragraphs that will include an introductory paragraph, a body of at least three paragraphs, and a concluding paragraph. The same format will apply to any writings such as e-mails, memos, letters, or reports.

The information we have learned thus far must have helped us a little to understand the format of the essay. Well! The above is not any different from the academic essay. Now, however, we need to acquire ample knowledge of what a paragraph is and what the characteristics that make an effective paragraph are. In the same manner, we need to acquire enough comprehension of what a thesis statement is and what makes it effective or ineffective.

We shall begin with the paragraph since it is the part of the whole.

The Paragraph

In short, a paragraph is the backbone or the building block of any piece of writing. It is a group of sentences that relate closely tone another and that address a single topic. This single topic we refer to as ***The Topic Sentence.*** To be effective, a paragraph should have a topic sentence that has one ***Controlling Idea***. An entire paragraph should involve itself with a distinct focus. This focus is the ***controlling idea*** in the ***topic sentence***.

Writing A Topic Sentence

Consistency makes the paragraph effortlessly plausible to a reader. It is the topic sentence that guides your paragraphs into harmony and soundness. It is the one *controlling idea* that you should satisfactorily develop and reinforce throughout your paragraph. Let us examine how this is done. Below, there are five core features to recall when writing a topic sentence.

Characteristics of the Effective Topic Sentence

1- A topic sentence must be a complete sentence.

2- A topic sentence must have ONE **controlling idea.**

3- The controlling idea must not be broad.

4- The controlling idea must not be too narrow.

5- The topic sentence must not be an announcement.

Now let us look at that in more detail:

1. The paragraph must have a topic sentence.

The topic sentence is the central part that links all the sentences in the paragraph. It shows the course the paragraph is taking. All sentences that follow the topic sentence should illuminate, describe, add proof, confirm, and advance the main idea.

Although a topic sentence may appear anywhere in the paragraph, I advise my students to write it at the beginning. This helps focus thoughts so that the sentences that follow may not stray from your main point.

"*One of the reasons that day was the most eventful in my life is that for the first time I missed an important exam.*"

In the above topic sentence, the controlling idea is "*missing and exam*" and we, hence, expect the details to focus on the how, why, the significance and the effect of that.

2. *Your topic sentence must include only one controlling idea.*

A controlling idea is the central idea of the paragraph. You will be discussing this one thing in your paragraph. For example, "*Cigarette smoking is hazardous to your health.*" While the topic of this sentence is cigarette smoking, the controlling idea is it being hazardous to your health. Note that a paragraph should have one idea only.

Just as the paragraph above, also, you will find that the controlling idea is only one and that is "***missing an important exam.***"

3. *Your topic sentence must not be too broad or too narrow.*

A broad controlling idea is one that cannot possibly be developed in one paragraph. If you write, for example, "***My College is a great place to attend.***" The controlling idea here "***great***" is so broad that you cannot possibly develop in one paragraph. In which way is it great? Surely in more than one way, thus, more paragraphs will be needed.

Here are some tips to help you write paragraphs. Although there are many items included in this list, you do not have to use all of them in every paragraph. Think about the topic of your essay and what you want to focus on in the paragraph. Then, use the tips that will help you achieve it.

CONSIDER THE FOLLOWING 73

- Use examples and illustrations.
- Avoid long sentences.
- Cite facts, statistics, or evidence.
- Examine what other people say with quotes and paraphrases.
- Use anecdotes or stories.
- Define terms in the paragraph.
- Compare or contrast ideas.
- Evaluate causes and reasons.
- Develop transitions to show relationships between sentences.
- Examine effects and consequences.
- Analyze or describe the topic or create a chronology of an event.

Here is a sample paragraph written by one of my students without my editing. The topic sentence is underlined:

CONSIDER THE FOLLOWING 74

"The movie "Beauty Knows No Pain" gives viewers an important message <u>about people should not be too selfish and eager for succeed</u>. This movie is produced by Lam Chi-wah. It describes two successful women in their life and career. One of the main characters is an ambitious woman, Jackie; she can do anything unscrupulously to achieve her goals. For example, one of the remarkable scenes was when she wanted to win a CEO position; she stole her best friend proposal, who was also her competitor in the contest. She was not only betrayed her friend, but she also gave up her boy friend to have her career. Even though she is very successful at the end, there is no one to share her success and joy. Hence, this movie is telling viewers that they should live generously and should not care too much about wining or losing, so that their life will be simpler and happier."

Here is a poorly written paragraph because it lacks logical and verbal bridges, which are important for the unity of the paragraph:

"In addition, my alarm did not go off on time and I was late getting to school on time. This was quite frustrating. The professor was upset and I was embarrassed."

CONSIDER THE FOLLOWING

Are you ready to write the paragraph? Let us give it a try?

Sit at your desk, take a deep breath and try to write a paragraph on any topic you enjoy thinking about. Go through the process you have learned: from brainstorming to clustering, to outlining, to creating a topic sentence that contains <u>ONE CONTROLLING IDEA</u> on the topic of your choice.

Here are some topic ideas to help you start.

- Music has changed a lot in recent years
- College education should be free.
- My college is the best college to attend.
- My college is the worst college to attend.
- The worst teacher I have ever had was ……
- The best teacher I have ever had was ….
- The government should do something about the deterioration of the environment.

There are many more you can think about. Remember, we are practicing writing a paragraph, so you need to focus on one controlling idea of these general topics.

Now, look again at the tips for writing a paragraph. How did you do?

Have you written a strong controlling idea in your topic sentence? Have you given ample example? Have you avoided using long, drawn-out sentences? Have you varied your sentences? Have you used transitions to develop connections between sentences? *If you answered, "yes" to the above questions, you have done marvelously well. If not, go back and revise your work. And remember, this is hard work that requires patience and persistence.*

In this struggle of learning to write well, and knowing that one must read well and a lot in order to write effectively, I am often reminded by the following quote by the prodigious Emily Dickinson:

"Reading is the resonance of ideas on the Soul's willing ear. It is a lonely mind through which the thoughts of another have not passed."

The Unmatched: Emily Dickinson

To sum this section on the topic sentence and the introductory paragraph, let us focus our thoughts a little more.

(1) The Five Paragraph Essay: Only when you have an understanding of the process and product, will these lessons on how to write introductory paragraphs make sense. Do you recall what I wrote that there is a trick to writing effectively in English? Well! Here it is. The outline below is the trick. You apply it to everything that you write about and just fill in the blanks using your creativity and knowledge.

It looks very much like the example I gave you above, but this will help instill the trick in your mind so that you could see that writing is not as difficult as you might have thought before reading this textbook. At any rate, one does not have to be *Albert Einstein* to be a brilliant writer.

Introduction: ------------------. ---------------------
. *Thesis Statement* ...idea 1. Idea 2..., idea 3....

First Supporting Paragraph: idea 1

Transition

Second Supporting Paragraph: idea 2

Transition

Third Supporting Paragraph: idea 3

Conclusion:

After-Thought:

(2) Initially and most importantly: Never struggle to write the whole essay as a final draft on first attempt.

(3) Start writing the introductory paragraph: Since the introductory paragraph is the most central since it introduces what your essay is about You have to seize the reader's attention with interest and clarity.

(4) Select your topic: about which you have enough information. Do some brainstorming to determine which the three best supporting ideas are. Now, consider and think about the point that you are trying to make. Think about the best words to use to convey this to your reader. Use active voice and avoid using passive voice, as it is much stronger that way. Be sure to write down each of these.

Now do the same thing for each of the three supporting ideas. Be sure that they are well written and explain a facet of the topic that you want to develop. Once you have that, there is just one more thing to write. It is the transitional words or phrases or a transition sentence that will connect these thoughts to your supporting paragraphs. Try to develop one sentence at a time.

(5) Once you have written all that review and take a second to look over that paragraph: Be sure that you have made it exciting to the reader. Be sure that the ideas flow easily one from the other and all your sentences are in order. The reader needs to see that there is connection. Unless you are writing a personal narrative, try not to use the pronoun "I." Make any corrections. When you are confident and happy with what you have accomplished, edit it again for errors.

(6) Never despair or be discouraged: with just one try. Write introductory paragraphs on many topics to practice and enhance your skill. The more you do it, the easier it gets.

(7) Take a break and walk away from writing: Put the introductory paragraphs that you have written aside and perhaps they can be developed later. Even if you do not later use them, they can be looked at for future essay writings. It is enjoyable to see a pattern of progress.

This is a quote by Victor Hugo that I like very much. Have it in mind.

"If a writer wrote merely for his time, I would have to break my pen and throw it away." Victor Hugo

Victor Hugo

CONSIDER THE FOLLOWING

Before we go into the *thesis statement*, here is a quick review and a reference for you on the writing of a *topic sentence*:

Paragraph's Ten Commandments

An essay consists of several paragraphs, each with a controlling idea and the details necessary to develop this idea. Hence, to write a well-organized, coherent and effective essay, you must be able to write organized, coherent and effective paragraphs. Does that make sense?

A paragraph is a group of sentences, which develop an idea. A paragraph in itself is an independent unit with its own purpose and focus. To present your audience with a clear and effective paragraph, you ought to observe certain guidelines.

1- **State the main idea of your paragraph in a topic sentence**:

   The topic sentence is the crucial part, which joins all the sentences in the paragraph together. It supplies the direction. All sentences that follow the topic sentence clarify. Explain, add evidence, reaffirm, and develop the main idea.
   Although a topic sentence may appear anywhere in the paragraph, and may even be implied (not stated), you are advised to write it at the beginning. Writing your topic sentence at the beginning helps you focus thoughts so that your sentences that follow may not deviate from your main point.

2- **Your topic sentence must include a controlling idea**:

   A controlling idea is the central idea of the paragraph. For example: Cigarette smoking is hazardous to your health. While the topic of this sentence is cigarette smoking, the controlling idea is hazardous to your health.

3- **Your topic sentence must not be too broad or too narrow**:

For example: *"Computers have changed our society."* This is too broad. *"The first car that I owned was a Ford."* This is too narrow.

4- **Each sentence in your paragraph must relate to the controlling idea:**

An irrelevant sentence confuses your reader and makes the purpose of your writing vague.

5- **Avoid long sentences**:

Writing short sentences helps you focus on your idea and helps prevent you from making errors or deviating from your point of focus.

6- **Use transitional devices**:

This will help show a relationship between your sentences.

7- **Avoid flowery words and wordiness**:

We will learn more about what flowery words and wordiness mean later in the text.

8- **Be short, precise, specific, and to the point:**

It is of utmost importance that your writing is focused and to the point. Try to be as specific as you can. English readers do not like long drawn writings, so try to be short and particular.

9- **Observe the logical relationship of cause and effect:**

If at any point of your writing you are making a cause and effect relationship, pay extra attention to this relationship and ensure that you are clear on what causes what to happen, or what the effects of something are.

10- **Pay attention to grammar:**

Of course, finally and most significantly, your grammar, verb tenses, verb forms and all the other elements of error-free writings ought be observed.

Note: It is important to remember that the purpose of writing, as with speaking, is to communicate information as clearly as possible. Don't try to impress your readers.

How are we doing so far? Now we are confident to move on to the thesis statement.

The Thesis Statement

As you would probably guess, the job of a thesis statement is to isolate the reason you are writing the essay. It, in a way, advertises the key ideas of the essay. Many languages state these key ideas at the end of writing; this would certainly confuse and irritate an English reader. In contrast to many other languages, when you write in English, you must explain the main point of your essay at the opening. You do this with the *thesis statement.*

Since the thesis statement is the most important statement in the whole essay, it must meet some prerequisites:

Rules for Effective Thesis Statements

Always use a complete sentence with a subject, verb, and complement.

Do not make it so broad that there is too much to write about.

Do not make it so narrow that there is too little to write about.

Keep it focused on the main topic.

Use a formal conversational tone; do not make it an announcement of the topic

In general, **do not use** qualifying statements that make the thesis depend on something specific, like your personal experiences or beliefs.
(Some essays, like narrative essays, may be about your personal experiences.)

Most of the time **write using** the third person; do not include first or second person terms. (Again, some essay styles will be an exception to this.)

Make the thesis statement the last sentence in the introductory paragraph.

Use the thesis statement as your point of reference, and refer to it continuously as you write your essay.

These seem to be many rules, however, most of them will be simple to monitor. Remember, though, that a thesis statement must apply all the above conditions. Now, we will see some examples of thesis statements so that you may have a good idea of how they are written:

Below are different thesis statements I have created. Some of these statements are effective; others are not. Try to write your own thesis statement based on the following question:

What are the advantages or disadvantages of online education?

Then, compare your writing to the ones I listed below. Do your best to create a convincing, well-defined, and specific thesis statement and follow all of the rules you have learned so far.

Example 1

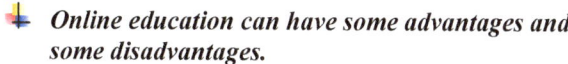
- ***Online education can have some advantages and some disadvantages.***

What is your opinion on this thesis statement? Do you think it can be effective? If you answered no, well done.

This is an example of a *vague thesis statement*, because it does not take a position. It states both sides of the situation, that there are advantages and disadvantages. It is difficult to write a linear essay if there are two opposing ideas. Do you think you can improve on it? Give it a try.

Here, I will suggest to you some possibilities of making it a more effective thesis statement.

Online education offers many advantages, such as freedom to choose when you want to learn and to learn from your home.

Online education has many disadvantages, such as too many choices and not having the chance to drive your new car.
Do you see the difference? These above two possible revisions show a more effective thesis that would help the reader know where the essay is going.

Example 2

🞣 **San Francisco has many tourist attractions and is a cosmopolitan city.**

What do you think? If your reply is not effective, you are right again. First, it has two key concepts (tourist attractions and a cosmopolitan city). Second, both of these ideas are not explicit enough. To make it more definite and unambiguous, you could list one or two kinds of tourist enticements. Or you could describe what makes San Francisco a multicultural city by citing its many theaters, cultural centers, or universities.

Do you see a pattern?

Here are more examples to help you further:

Example 3

🞣 *I want to write about ways to maintain health.*

At first glance, one might conclude that this thesis statement is effective. If you take a closer look at how it begins. The words "*I want to write* . . ." make this an announcement. You must avoid announcing what you will write about or what your paper will address. You could also see that there is another problem with the sentence, which is in the second, the phrase "***ways to maintain health.***" The phrase is too broad because surely there are many, many ways to maintain health; the writer is not specific enough.

To make this a more effective and workable thesis statement, I would have to identify three specific ways for people to maintain health. Another possible way of revising this sentence is to select one method to maintain health, and then develop three main points about it.

Here are two examples I created:

Some major ways to maintain health are to exercise daily, eat seven servings of colorful vegetables each day, and get at least eight hours of sleep each night.

Colorful vegetables and fruits, like squash, cabbage, and berries, contain high levels of vitamins and minerals to help you maintain your health.

So, do you feel more confident now about how to create an effective and a workable thesis statement? I hope you do.

Do you remember when I wrote, "It is a trick?" – Well! This is part the trick, too, in addition to the outline and all the other elements we discussed so far.

Once you have a thesis statement, the next step is to create the introductory paragraph. Here are the steps you can take to write this very important component of an essay.

Introductory Paragraphs

Introductory paragraphs are central because they are the first part your reader reads. If a reader is not taken by the introduction, he or she will not continue reading. However, if the reader finds the introduction appealing, operational, and well written, he or she will continue reading the essay with attention.

Watching a movie and reading an essay are very similar. Have you ever walked out from a movie theater shortly after the movie started? I have done so many times, sometimes after only 10 or 15 minutes. The first 10 minutes of a movie are like the introductory paragraph of your essay. If people read the introductory paragraph of your essay and do not like it, they will simply stop reading.

Let me tell you a secret about teachers. Teachers develop an immediate opinion of the writer's skills after reading only the introductory paragraph. If the student does not write a strong, organized, and coherent introduction, the teacher will automatically decide that the student lacks writing skills and will grade the essay unfavorably because of this developed bias. If, on the other hand, the introductory paragraph is thrilling, stimulating and well written, the teacher will have a favorable opinion of the writer and will read the essay more carefully. That is my opinion based on my experiences sitting on committees that read essay exams.

Essay writers should be very careful and pay extra attention to their introductory paragraphs. It is sensible to spend extra time to cautiously prepare your introductory paragraphs. When they are clear, succinct, sound, and free of errors, you will have a better chance of getting a high score on your essay. Here are steps you can take to write an appealing introductory paragraph.

After you choose the topic of your essay and write your thesis statement, you begin your introductory paragraph. It will include two or three sentences that introduce the topic you are addressing. You can use your introductory paragraph to describe ideas or give examples to help your reader appreciate the thesis statement.

CONSIDER THE FOLLOWING

For example, let us say you are writing about cultures. Your essay will focus on the unwritten cultural rules that regulate people's behavior. To help readers understand these topics, you should define *culture* and give examples of it in the two or three sentences that come before your thesis statement.

Here is an example of an introduction written by one of my students on the topic of cultures:

> *One part of defining a culture is when a group of people voluntarily agrees on doing something together and they let a code of unwritten rules develop to guide their activities. Such rules might also include decisions on how to deal with those who breach cultural unwritten rules. Chinese culture is at least 5,000 years old, and one could say that the cultural rules there are very strong. There are three unwritten rules that play an important role in regulating behavior in China: the first rule relates to the concept of saving face; the second rule relates to the role each individual must play in society as a whole; and the third rule is the respect one must give the elderly.*

Here you may easily notice that the first three sentences lead readers right to the thesis. The first sentence defines an over-all classification of culture. Next, the second sentence points out one specific component of culture. The third sentence introduces a specific culture (Chinese) and leads readers right to the thesis statement in the fourth sentence.

Do you find this information motivating? Even if you do not enjoy the topic, did you clearly understand what this essay was about? This student did an excellent job of writing clear sentences that help readers understand the thesis statement and where the essay is going.

I wish to encourage you not be too concerned about making mistakes or finding the process of writing troublesome. We all learn from our mistakes and we improve that way. This reminds me of a great quote by James Joyce:

"Mistakes are the portals of discovery."
- James Joyce

Writer James Joyce

Now it is time to move on to the final two components of an essay—the body and the conclusion.

Knowledge Is Power

The Body of the Essay

There is no established recipe or list of rules for the body of an essay. Simply, in the body of the essay, you sway, encourage, or educate your readers. In the traditional academic five-paragraph essays, the body of an essay is made up of three paragraphs. In these three paragraphs you write your topic sentence (from your already developed outline), and develop each of the details from that point. When you write the body of your essay, check the paragraphs against the thesis statement in general and the topic sentence of each paragraph in particular to make sure they link and correlate.

As in all the other paragraphs, the body paragraphs must have a topic sentence each and at least three other sentences that support it. Each topic sentence should be taken directly from the already developed thesis statement. As it is always the rule, well-defined language, correct grammar, no spelling errors, and complete sentences or independent clauses are essential to make these paragraphs strong, clear, and focused.

CONSIDER THE FOLLOWING

The Conclusion of the Essay

The conclusion paragraph is where you will wrap up your essay and bring your reader back to the thesis statement. There are two things to be accomplished in a conclusion. First, a writer reminds the readers of the main points of the thesis statement paraphrasing it, of course. Second, the reader needs to see how all the different details in the body of the essay relate to the thesis statement. Now the essay is logical, coherent and comprehensible.

Below are two examples of thesis statements and their conclusions.

Example 1:

> Online education offers many advantages, such as freedom to choose when you want to learn, where you want to learn, and how much you have to pay to learn.

Conclusion:

> When you are looking for different methods to improve your knowledge or learn something new, online education is the perfect winner. Instead of having to go to a classroom at a certain time on certain days, you can attend an online class whenever you have the time and in the comfort of your own home. No more braving bad weather to make it to class by the late bell! Most important, you don't have to break the bank to pay for this education. The future of education is online. So do not get left behind.

CONSIDER THE FOLLOWING 96

Example 2:

    In the world today, poverty is a hurdle to many things for the women of South Africa, impacting their health, education, and safety.

Conclusion:

>One woman' story of illness is told every day throughout South Africa. Though medical help is slowly arriving, it may not be in time to save her or her children. Another woman wants to earn more money to help her children attend school, but after rebels destroyed her village's crops, she can do little because she cannot read or write. Her children now beg in the streets just to get enough to feed themselves. Those same rebels who destroyed the village's crops did more damage to a third woman who fears the outside world that surrounds her. When poverty is removed, we will see the desolation and obliteration reduced and, hopefully, abolished.

So, you now have all the components of the essay written: introductory paragraph with the thesis statement, three body paragraphs, and one conclusion paragraph.

Do you think you are finished? If you are like all careful writers who want to do their best, then your answer would be no.

Chapter Six: Writing Consideration

We have now developed the foundation for our ability to write coherently and effectively. We understand the principles and the "tricks" of the writing process from its beginning to its conclusion. Though this is the most important, there are still other considerations to make writings smooth and readable.

The first thing we will cover here is the stage after writing the first draft. Once the first draft has been completed, we now need to revise and edit our work.

Revising and Editing

Revising is a critical step in the writing process. This is when you give an ultimate form to your writing and polish what you are providing your readers. Going through this process, you ought to check for any spelling, grammar, or punctuation errors.

A word of caution here: Do not depend on Microsoft Word Program for checking your spelling, grammar or punctuation; it is not always accurate. You may use it as a first step, but you must manually check your writing carefully for errors.

College students who are attending writing classes may find that most teachers allow students to revise their papers. If you are a student, take this step seriously because it is the final fate of your writing; here you may alter the content a little if you find necessary.

Once you have completed this revising stage, the next step is to edit your writing.

I prefer to start editing by inspecting the effectiveness of the transitions between ideas and between paragraphs and ensure flow. Next, I make sure that I have developed my ideas adequately. I also examine the supporting information such as details, illustrations and examples, to ensure it relates to the thesis statement in general and to each topic sentence in each paragraph in particular.

A writer must also closely scrutinize sentence structure, watch for the clarity of word choices, and eliminate fragments, run-on sentences, comma splices, and clichés (all of which we will elaborate upon later in the textbook). Finally, it is very important to check for grammatical errors with verb tenses, subject-verb agreement, and plural and singular nouns. Only at this point that whatever you are writing is in its final draft and ready for your reader's valuation.

Does that make sense to you? Are you anxious because you are not acquainted with some of the terms I just listed? You do not have to be, because we will discuss those terms in more detail now.

Choosing the Right Word

Not only ESL/EFL learners have difficulties with selecting the right word, but also native speakers do. However, as ESL/EFL learners, we face interference from our native languages. This is especially true if our native language encourages wordiness and flowery words in writing. We might find ourselves writing more words in English than we need to or use figurative language that sound awkward in English and would lose power in translation.

The famous American writer **Mark Twain** once said,

"If you find an adjective, kill it."

When I started learning English, I often used many words to describe something. In Arabic, my native language, it is customary, acceptable, and perhaps expected and encouraged that writers use many words.

This was a problem for me because English readers prefer concise and straight writing that is free of replication. They want clean, uncluttered writing. So, I want to help you avoid the mistakes I used to make. When you write, make it a point to select your words sensibly and wisely remembering always that you are writing in English and for English readers.

I am reminded again of another quote by the great writer Mark Twain. He wrote:

"*We write frankly and fearlessly but then we "modify" before we print.*"

The Great Mark Twain

How to Clip Wordiness

College students are sometimes under pressure to write a certain number of words, such as when an instructor asks you to write a 500-word essay. Personally, I reject that approach; however, many professors still demand it. Students often feel pressured about writing so many words, so instead of developing ideas fully, they may cushion their writings with unnecessary expressions and locutions to reach the word count. This, however, will not help the effectiveness of writing neither will it help improving grades. On the contrary, it will hurt and make writing look superficial. Teachers want to see essence, not hollow fillers.

So, if you can say what you want to say in one word, write it in one word. Let me show you an example. Avoid phrases such as *"The student with great success."* It is much more effective to say, *"The successful student."* Both phrases are grammatically correct, but when you are writing an essay in English, the second is preferred because it precise, concise, and to the point.

Here is a list of wordy expressions you could replace with the single word, "***Because***," and you should make an effort to avoid using:

- The reason for
- For the reason that
- Due to the fact that
- In light of the fact that
- Considering the fact that
- On the grounds that
- This is why

CONSIDER THE FOLLOWING

The word "***When***" can easily replace these next phrases:

- On the occasion of
- In a situation in which
- Under circumstances in which

Finally, which single word do you think can replace these phrases?

- Is able to
- Has the opportunity to
- Has the capacity for
- Has the ability to

If you said, "***Can***", you are correct! You understand the idea now.

Wordiness can appear anywhere in your essay. As writers, we all have to be cautious and pay extra attention to this matter as it causes the reader irritation and discomfort. Readers want to read short, concise, and succinct information. They do not have time to guess what the writer is trying to do or why the writer is doing what she or her is doing.

Below is a list of phrases used by learners often when writing thesis statements or creating supporting details. To the right of the phrases are suggestions on how to revise them.

Wordy Phrase	Revised Phrase
• At the present time	• Now
• In the event that	• If
• In the near future	• Soon
• Due to the fact that	• Because
• For the reason that	• Because
• Is able to	• Can
• In every instant	• Always
• In this day and age	• Today
• During the time that	• While
• A large number of	• Many
• Return back	• Return
• Commute back and forth	• Commute

We must remember that using pointless words in writing is not effective. If we can say what we want to say in one word, we should do it in one word. My experience has taught me that it is much better to use the one word! Let me share with you an example from one of my students:

> *"In my essay, I am going to describe why at the present time I am so much against capital punishment and want the government to get rid of it."*

In addition to being an announcement, which one should not do, what is the first thing you see wrong? It has many unnecessary words that do not serve any purpose. It would have been more effective had that student reduced the sentence to the following:

"Capital punishment should be abolished."

Do you know how I arrived at that reduced sentence? The reason this is better is that it is stronger and succinct. Extra words irritate and confuse the reader and can make the reader blunder the main point the writer is attempting to make.

CONSIDER THE FOLLOWING 106

Eliminating Repetition

At first you might think that "repetitive meaning" refers to using the same word again and again and again (like I just did here). Even though it is true you do not want to use the same word several times with no reason (sometimes writers do it for special effect), This is something very different. The repetition here is not about wording but about meaning. This problem is also called redundancy. It might be a lot easier for you to understand this concept if I use examples.

Here is something that will possibly make you smile. First, read the following phrases. Then, think about each of them for a minute or two.

- Red in color
- Of cheap quality
- Honest in character
- In a confused state
- Unusual in nature
- Extreme in degree
- Of a strange type
- Large in size
- Oftentimes
- Heavy in weight
- Period in time
- Round in shape

What do you think? Did you smile? If you smiled, why did you? Do you see the repetition-taking place in each of the phrases? If not, here is some more explanation. Let us choose three of these phrases. First is **red in color**. If you use the word red to describe an object, then your reader already knows you are talking about color. Therefore, you do not need the words in color. Does that make sense?

Next, let us look at ***large in size***. If something is large, then it is clear you are referring to its size.

Last, consider ***heavy in weight***. The word heavy tells your readers that you referring to weight, right?

So, in these phrases, the only words that are necessary are red, large, and heavy. You can take out the extra words that are repetitive in meaning in each of the phrases above.

CONSIDER THE FOLLOWING

Pretentious and Flowery Words

As I mentioned above, for ESL/EFL learners, native language interferes in learning a new language. Some of our native languages encourage flowery words in writing. Furthermore, there are some other writers feel they can improve their writing by using decorative, and extravagant words rather than unpretentious, natural words. They use unnatural language that more often obscures their meaning than communicates it clearly. Here are some overblown words we ought to avoid and replace with simpler words:

Shakespeare, the Master

Pretentious Words	Simple Words
Finalize	Finish
Transmit	Send
Facilitate	Help
Component	Part
Initiate	Begin
Delineate	Describe
Manifested	Shown

In my experience as a journalist and a writing instructor, I have encountered articles and essays in which the writers felt they could improve their writing by using big, fancy words and long sentences. Writers like these want to impress their readers by showing their vocabulary power.

They fail to understand, however, that using artificial, inflated words makes it hard for the reader to understand and impedes clear communication. In writing this textbook, I must admit, I may be guilty of that because of my native language interference.

Academically, we refer to inflated and unnatural words and expressions as ***pretentious or flowery words***. When writing, you need to avoid using pretentious words if you want to communicate clearly with your readers.

CONSIDER THE FOLLOWING

Vague Words

In all writing, we must not use any generic word whose meaning is not well defined. Take the word **good** for example, what does it really mean? The dictionary takes nearly an entire column to capture its many definitions. Words such as **good, bad, and wonderful are vague** and do not describe exactly what the writer wants to describe.

For example, if we write, "**Hawaii is a wonderful place**," our readers will not understand what exactly we mean by **wonderful**. Is the weather wonderful? Is the scenery wonderful? Is the food wonderful? Are the people wonderful? How is it wonderful? Is it exciting, peaceful, fun? Do you see what I mean? A writer needs to be as accurate and exact as he or she possibly can.

Here is one way we could clarify that sentence: "**Hawaii's hidden waterfalls take you to a magical, primeval world**."

Take the time, then, to know just what you want to communicate. Do not start writing before you start thinking.

Confusing Words

English can be such a tricky language. There are so many words that sound alike but whose spelling and meaning are very different. We also see words that are spelled the same but can have two or more different meanings. Finally, we will see how putting two negative words together will flip the sentence's meaning to something positive. Now, how tricky is that? Even native English speakers sometimes have trouble with these, so I want you to be very patient and be very proud of yourself.

Homophones and Homonyms

Many spelling or word-choice errors are caused by words known as homophones and homonyms. This happens often if a writer depends on Microsoft Word Programs to correct errors; such programs are not able to identify the differences. **Homophones** are two or more words that are pronounced the same but have different spellings and meanings. On the other hand, *homonyms* are spelled the same but have different meanings.

To choose the right word and spell it correctly, you need to depend on the connotation of the sentence you write. Again, I cannot stress this enough, do not rely on your computer to correct such words for you.

Below are lists, one for homophones and one for homonyms. These lists signify words that you will use regularly in your writing. You will find it valuable to make an effort to learn and distinguish them.

Homophones	
Ant (insect)	Aunt (sibling of your mother or father)
Beat (to hit)	Beet (a vegetable)
Blew (past tense of verb *to blow*)	Blue (color)
Capital (assets)	Capitol (government building)
Flew (past tense of verb *to fly*)	Flu (illness)
Groan (a sound made when in pain)	Grown (past tense of the verb *to grow*)
Hole (an opening)	Whole (entire)
Know (knowledge of something)	No (opposite of yes)

CONSIDER THE FOLLOWING

Here are a few sentences that will show you how these words are used in the English language:

- *I found ants crawling around in my bathroom.*
- *Sabri's aunt is a pianist in Las Vegas.*
- *Mary just flew on an airplane from London Paris.*
- *Scientists say that the flu season this year will be very bad.*
- *I know who you are.*
- *You are no friend of mine.*

Reading is the Food of the Mind and Soul

Homonyms		
	First meaning	Second meaning
Bank	Place to save money	Side of a river
Bust	To break something	Sculpture of a head
Cabinet	Cupboard	Advisers to president
Cable	A strong piece of rope or wire	Television channels you must pay for
Cage	To restrain or confine	A box or enclosure
Date	Specific day	Fruit

CONSIDER THE FOLLOWING

Here are a few more sentences that will show you how these words are used in the English language:

>I need to deposit money in the **bank** on the corner.
>Otters dig holes in the **bank** of this river.
>
>Jared ate candy apples and hot dogs at the **fair**.
>The terms of the agreement seem **fair**, and both parties are happy with them.
>
>Kim was sick today and had to **lie** down on the couch for two hours.
>You cannot **lie** about eating the cookies—I see crumbs on your lips!

CONSIDER THE FOLLOWING

Watch for Double Negative

People, native and non-native speakers alike, commonly make mistakes with double negatives. Although some languages allow double negatives in some circumstances, English does not. In fact, a double negative cancels out the negative and creates a positive statement. It is like math in that way. See the sentence below:

The student was <u>not unhappy</u> with his grades.

The double negative in this sentence is ***<u>not unhappy</u>***. This phrase means that the student was happy. Do you see how that works in English? Remember that the negative words such as *no*, *not*, or *never* should not accompany other negative modifiers or negative expressions such as *nothing*, *nobody*, or words that begin with *-un-*

How are you doing so far? Is all of this making sense? I know this is too much information, but gradually you will grasp all and with practice, you will feel more confident and find the process as well as the knowledge to be entertaining.

Now we move to a different rule in writing and that is to avoid slang language and clichés. It is not uncommon that novice writers cannot distinguish between what and what is not slang, especially now with the media using slang language all the time. However, in formal writing, slang is fawned upon and is certainly unacceptable in any academic environment.

Avoid Using Slang and Clichés

First, let us look at slang. Slang refers to popular, awfully informal words or phrases. These have no place in formal or academic writing. Some of the slang words and phrases that my students have used include the following:

- Freak me out
- Let's split
- Veg out
- The idiot box
- Get it together
- Shove off
- Rip off
- Stuffed
- Gross me out

Now let me show you some sentences that use these terms. Some are very silly, so it is okay to laugh!

*When we told the neighbors **to can the noise**, they freaked out.*

*I didn't know how **messed** up John was until he stole money from his parents and **split**.*

*After a hard day, I **like to veg out** in front of **the idiot box**.*

*Andrew was so **wiped out** after his workout at the gym that he couldn't **get it together** to defrost a frozen dinner.*

*When Paul tried to **put the moves** on Maria, she told him to **shove off**.*

*My father claims that most **grease monkeys are rip-off** artists.*

> *After the game, we **stuffed our faces** at the dinner.*
>
> *The horror movie **grossed me out**.*

Perhaps you do not even know some of these words. It is okay if you do not! You are one of the lucky learners. However, if you do and you are tempted to use them in your writing, do not.

Below is a table that lists proper alternatives to the slang terms I just listed.

Proper Alternatives to Slang Terms	
Slang Term	**Proper Term**
Let's split	Let us leave
Veg out	Relax
Idiot box	Television
Get it together	Focus
Shove off	Leave
Rip off	Steal

Choose your words sensibly when you write. Improve the habit of selecting words that are exact and suitable for your purpose. You must circumvent slang if you want your essay (or any of your writing) to sound intelligent and professional. This idea is connected to knowing your audience. The professors or work managers who read your writings will not like to see you use any of these terms.

CONSIDER THE FOLLOWING

About Clichés

A cliché is a term whose meaning has been overused. Although clichés are common in speech, they make writing seem dull. You should avoid clichés and try to express your meaning in creative ways. Here are some typical clichés to watch out for:

- Short but sweet
- Last but not least
- Work like a dog
- It dawned on me
- All work and no play
- On top of the world
- In the nick of time
- Too close for comfort
- Easier said than done
- Too little, too late
- Time and time again
- Make ends meet
- It goes without saying
- Word to the wise
- At a loss for words

It may take you a little more time to think of a fresh way of saying something, but it is sure to be better than using a tiresome cliché. After all, any tiresome phrases could make your essay itself look tiresome, when it certainly is not. So, try to be as specific and precise as you can with what you want to say. That is the best way to avoid clichés.

Now we move to grammar and verbs and their rules – Are we ready?

A great quote by Louisa May Alcott reflects the truth of our lives. She wrote:

"Life is like college; may I graduate and earn some honors."

Writer Louisa May Alcott

Again, please do not be afraid to make mistakes, as we learn from them. I remember another great quote by George Bernard Shaw. He wrote:

"A life spent in making mistakes is not only more honorable but more useful than a life spent doing nothing."

The Great Bernard Shaw

Chapter Seven:

The Importance of Grammar in Writing

Gerunds and Infinitives

Whether to end a verb in *-ing* or start it with *to* is a trouble spot for the ESL learner. We often wonder whether we should use a *gerund*, as in *working, sleeping, studying*; or an *infinitive*, as in *to work, to sleep, or to study*. It may be a better idea to begin with gerunds.

Even though a gerund is the *-ing* form of a verb, it is not a verb at all; it is a noun. Remember for future reference that a **gerund can be a verb only if it is preceded by the verb *to be*.** Therefore, we need to remember that a gerund standing alone functions as a noun. **A test for gerunds is to replace the noun with the pronoun *it*.** Let us look at an example:

Reading enhances our ability to write.

What is the verb in this sentence? If you answer *enhances*, you are correct. In this case, **reading is the subject of the sentence. It is a noun.** How do we know? We can **replace *reading* with the pronoun *it*,** and the sentence will still be correct:

It enhances our ability to write.

In this way, you know that *reading* is a noun gerund, and it is not a verb at all, as many new learners might think.

On the other hand, an *infinitive* is the verb preceded by *to*. Think of it as the clearest form of the verb in its untouched and unmodified form. An infinitive cannot be a noun because it is an action. **Our test for infinitives is to replace the action verb with the verb *to do*.** In the sentence above, *our ability to write* means our ability *to do it*.

This distinction has always worked for me. When you are in doubt as to whether to use a gerund or an infinitive, ask yourself if you can substitute the pronoun *it* or the action *to do it*. If you can use *it*, a gerund will be correct. If you must use *to do it*, an infinitive should be your choice.

Let us try it. Complete the following sentence using the word *write*:

        I enjoy _____.

To choose the right form, ask whether you can say, ***I enjoy it*** or ***I enjoy to do it***. The response is: **I enjoy** *it*

   Therefore, the sentence should be,
   I enjoy writing.

Here is a list of verbs that are followed by gerunds:

- Admit
- Appreciate
- Avoid
- Deny
- Enjoy
- Finish
- Miss
- Postpone
- Practice
- Quit
- Recall
- Resist
- Suggest

CONSIDER THE FOLLOWING

Here is a list of verbs that are followed by infinitives:

- Agree
- Ask
- Claim
- Decide
- Expect
- Have

- Hope
- Manage
- Offer
- Plan
- Pretend
- Promise

- Refuse
- Wait
- Want
- Wish

Here are verbs that can be followed by either an infinitive or a gerund:

- Begin
- Continue

- Hate
- Like

- Love
- Start

Try using these verbs to get a sense of how they function. We need a lot of practice.

CONSIDER THE FOLLOWING

Reported Speech

To report a speech that was said in the past, you need to use the next level of the past tense of that verb. For example, the original statement

She said, "My name is Maria."

It should be reported as,

She said her name was Maria.

Notice that the verb *is* in Maria's original statement is changed to "***was***" in our reported statement.

The key rule to remember about reported speech is that the verb in the speech you heard *must be changed to the next level of the past tense*. The present will change to the past, and the past will change to the past perfect. For example, if someone said,

I went to the movies.

You would need to report this as,

He said he had gone to the movies.

Again, notice that *went*, which is the past tense, changed to: ***had gone***, which is **the past perfect tense**. Many speakers ignore this rule, but to be correct as, you should not.

Here is a great quote by the marvelous Jean-Jacques Rousseau. He wrote:

"To write a good love letter, you ought to begin without knowing what you mean to say, and to finish without knowing what you have written."

The Marvelous Jean Jacques Rousseau

CONSIDER THE FOLLOWING 129

Chapter Eight: The Types Of Essay Questions

Now we are in real life situations where you will actually be asked to write an essay; that is if you are a college student. If you are a working adult, it is the same thing: you may be asked to write a memo, a report, an email message, a formal letter or even an essay. The format, as indicated earlier in this textbook, is just the same and the rules are also the same.

However, for our purpose, we shall focus on the types of essay questions that might be asked of you as a college learner.

Later, in the next chapter, when we study the different essay modes, you will make more sense of this. In most cases, you might be asked to write essays of five-paragraphs or even longer if you have to write a term paper or a book review.

- The essay questions focus on these possible areas:
- To describe something
- To recount a story or an event or events
- To compare something to another
- To contrast something against another
- To write a formal letter
- To show a relationship of cause and effect
- To illustrate something
- To describe a process
- To review a book or books
- To review a film
- To write a short story
- To write about yourself
- To argue for or against a controversial topic

Whatever the question is, you will still need to follow the guidelines we have learned and you will still go through the process of writing we learned in Chapter Three. To remind you, here again is *the outline format*:

CONSIDER THE FOLLOWING

The Writing Process

1. Prewriting
2. Outlining
3. Writing
4. Revising
5. Editing

I. **Introduction**

- The Topic
- The Thesis (or the main idea)

II. **First Idea**

- Idea
- Details

III. **Second Idea**

- Idea
- Details

IV. **Third Idea**

- Idea
- Details

V. **Conclusion**

- Restating the Thesis Statement
- Writing an Afterthought

Sample Outline for Writing an Essay

NOTE

I hope you are liking reading this: "CONSIDER THE FOLLOWING: WRITING FROM A NON-NATIVE PERSPECTIVE."

Remember, English is my third language (unnatural, remember?) – I would like that you will notice that in the editing stage, we see and read what we think it is, and not what it actually is. This is referred to as "Miscue," in linguistics. Be more careful than I have been with the editing stage.

Introduction: ------------------. ------------
----------. *Thesis Statement* ...idea 1. Idea 2..., idea 3....

First Supporting Paragraph: idea 1

Transition

Second Supporting Paragraph: idea 2

Transition

Third Supporting Paragraph: idea 3

Conclusion:

After-Thought:

Thinking of writing most of the time, doing it and teaching it, I cannot help but remembering various quotes of great writers, not only on life and living, but on writing and the writing process. Now, the incomparable Oscar Wilde reminds me. He wrote,

"I was working on the proof of one of my poems all the morning, and took out a comma. In the afternoon I put it back again."

The Incomparable Oscar Wilde

Chapter Nine:

The Most Important Types of Essays

Writer Jonathan Swift

CONSIDER THE FOLLOWING

Descriptive, Narrative, and Explanatory Essays

Under each of these categories, you will find many different styles of essay writing. For instance, under descriptive, you can use the chronological style or the compare and contrast style. It's also important to know that some styles fit into more than one of the three general essay categories. Below you'll see the different styles of writing and which essay categories they fit in.

Descriptive	Narrative	Explanatory
Chronological	Chronological	Definition
Compare and Contrast	Process	Example
Example	Analysis	Process
Process		Analysis

For now, we will focus on the three essay categories.

The essay category you choose will depend on the assignment you are given or what your task is, the topic of your writing, and how you want to communicate with your audience. Do you have to describe a famous person in the news for your essay? Do you want to write about a personal experience? Do you want your audience to understand the similarities between two things? These are just a few of the questions you need to answer before you choose the type of essay category you will use.

It is important for any writer to know these categories and when to use them. Each one has its own format, organization, and use. So, let us begin. We will first discuss *descriptive essays.*

CONSIDER THE FOLLOWING

The Descriptive Essay

This is a very important category because it is used the most when writing essay. Regardless of the writing style you choose, all descriptive essays have three characteristics:

1. They have a particular, well-defined, and central tone. You tell your readers exactly what you think—if you support or do not support an idea. As you write the essay, you will use this to guide you when choosing the specifics you will include.

2. Descriptive essays can be objective or subjective. (Objective is when you describe things without adding your personal feelings or opinions. Subjective is when you describe something based on your own experiences or opinions.)

Descriptive essays assist the reader to picture the subject of your essay and become engaged in what you are describing. You use adjectives and adverbs to bring your essay to life for the reader.

CONSIDER THE FOLLOWING

How to Write a Descriptive Essay

There is no single method that will help you create the precise descriptive essay every time. How you write it will depend on the subject of your essay and what you want to reveal to your readers. In writing a descriptive essay, you must sensibly select your details. It is these details that will help your readers visualize what you are unfolding.

Think about *the five senses: sight, sound, taste, touch*, and *smell*. When you think about what you want to say and the details you will use, try to think about the five senses of your readers. So, when they read your essay, all their senses will be used. You may find that a descriptive essay very often relies on the feelings of the reader to communicate its point.

To begin this essay, try giving all the details first; then, build your description from these details. If you are writing about a historical event, give the date, the location, the people who are involved, and any fact that your reader needs to understand the point of your essay.

Examine your details to be sure that they are uniform with the thesis statement you created.

Then, use the details to move your reader through the essay. The introductory paragraph is your starting point. From there, take the readers to the next logical step in the process, remembering to always refer to your outline and your thesis statement to steer you. No matter what writing style you use for this essay, you need to keep your details focused.

Now let's take a look at an example of a descriptive essay. We will use the outline we created for Disneyland in an earlier lesson. Here is the thesis statement of an essay written by one of my students: *Living in New York.* Please note that the essay has been graded and I have some comments on it. You might find these comments helpful, too.

CONSIDER THE FOLLOWING

Descriptive Essay Example:

Written by One of My College Students

I miss the days of sitting in my living room nestled in my thick wool blanket as I listened to the loud sounds throughout the night. I would play the game of "Guess Where That Sound is coming from" with the other girls who lived in the group home. In the "Bush", you could hear the sounds of loud screaming from drunken club goers as they return home off the bus which WChoice 1 -WHOSE- brakes you could hear screeching from three blocks away. Every five minutes there were new sounds, but those sounds were not as common as the loud pop that came from a 44-caliber pistol. This was just another night in the hood, and these were the sounds that comforted me as I put the day to rest.

Growing up in a group home in East Flatbush, Brooklyn New York had its advantages because of the diverse and rich culture, which attracted all types of people from around the world. In my eyes, I had the entire world right in my backyard, and there was never a reason to leave the Bush because everything you ever needed could be found in the Bush. Every day on my way to school I passed the roti shop and always ordered the same thing- palori—CLARITY PROBLEM- with ginger beer on the side to wash it down. It was a ritual for me after school to walk nine blocks home with the girls from the group home with whom I was a friend, and they were the family I never had. Each day on the way home Punctuation COMMA- we found a different hot dog vendor to purchase hot dogs from. I always paid for mine while my sisters found a way to distract the vendors and run off once they had the hot dog in their hands because they would do anything to save up their dollars so that they can purchase the latest Lisa album. Coming home was never a treat because we would have to walk through "Little Jamaica", which got its name because of all the high population of Jamaican emigrants that migrated to this particular part of Brooklyn; they were the ones that would kill to make it in America.

The evenings were always a fun time after we finished eating dinner because we hung out <u>Avoid Using Slang Language</u> in the back yard listening to the cattle calls of the neighborhood boys as they tried to get our attention so that we could sneak them inside the house. The most exciting time of the day was the night when we would curl up in our blankets, turn down the lights, and crouch down low into the couches. Listening to the sounds of the Bush was far more exciting than watching television because this was real life, and the closest thing to that were the television shows "Cops" and "Americas Most Wanted". When the sirens started to sing we played our game, "Guess What That Noise Is" and "Is It Murder or a Fire", and if we heard people screaming, we would try to guess if it was a drug dealer doing business, partygoers that just got robbed or loud music. Whatever the noises were, we always knew that majority of the time they were always associated with something negative; flashing lights with loud sirens were my lullabies back then.

No matter how many times I used to hear it, I could never get used to it, yet I found the sound of a 44 magnum to be the most comforting sound of them all. It reminded me of sweet memories regardless of the bitter consequences. The Jamaicans were known for being the local drug dealers of the neighborhood in East Flatbush, so whenever we heard the loud popping sounds from a gun we knew that it was the Jamaicans handling their business. This night was no different than the other nights when we heard the loud screeching of the B63 bus as it came to its stop or the drunken partygoers as they exited the bus. This night was the night that the normal became scary as we crouched down into our seats and heard one man soon after the loud popping sounds of a gun and a woman yelling for help. This was a scary way to live life, but this was the only way that I knew how to live, and this was my home in my world.

It has been years since I have lived in East Flatbush, and it almost feels like another lifetime to me, but I miss my lullabies that would comfort me as I put the day to rest. The Bush will always be my home and every time I hear a Jamaican accent, smell a hot dog with roasted onions, or hear the loud popping sounds of a gun I feel comforted, and I feel home sick. Now I live in the Rose Garden neighborhood of San Jose where

I find it difficult to sleep because my lullabies have been replaced by barking dogs, children crying, and the music that comes from the Mexican tap dancing school. These are all new and wonderful noises to hear, but they do not soothe me, in fact; they keep me up at night. I look forward to my next trip home as I long to be comforted.

Can you guess the writing style my student used for this essay? It is the example style. Using outline he took the main point of the thesis statement (This was just another night in the hood, and these were the sounds that comforted me as I put the day to rest) and used examples to describe this idea.

In the first body paragraph, he discussed growing up in New York. For the next body paragraph, he explained his evenings living there; then he continued to describe how he could never get used to the violence therein his conclusion, he surprises the readers by stating that he still misses it and remembering the positive sides of having lived there.

My student's essay reminds me of the great writer Virginia Woolf who wrote:

"If you do not tell the truth about yourself you cannot tell it about other people."

The Great Virginia Woolf

CONSIDER THE FOLLOWING

The Narrative Essay

I think it is fun to write narrative essays. After all, it is most like telling a good story. For you, what makes a good story? Is it the enthusiasm and excitement of the storyteller? Is it the words he uses? Or is it how she focuses on just the right details to make the story move forward in a logical order? These are just a few things that make a good story. They will help you write a good narrative essay, too.

To *narrate* means to tell a story. A narrative essay details a story of an event or an experience that has left an effect on the person telling it. When you write a narrative essay, your main task is to capture the interest of your readers. Some of you might have read Helen Keller's narrative ***The Story of My Life***. Although it is not an essay, it is a classic example of what a narrative story is.

In order to write an effective narrative essay, you must first have an important tale to tell. You must include all the important details that lead to the event, and you must show the effect of the event. Be sure that you do all this in chronological and logical order.

Be careful writing your details. While you will need to include all the important and significant events that make up the story, do not bore your reader with irrelevant information that has no bearing on the meaning or the purpose of the story.

Let us first read Helen Keller's story *"The Story of My Life,"* which is fortunately in **public domain,** so we can all enjoy Keller's magic. Then we will learn how to write a narrative essay.

The Story of My Life

Helen Keller

Chapter IV

The most important day I remember in all my life is the one on which my teacher, Anne Mansfield Sullivan, came to me. I am filled with wonder when I consider the immeasurable contrasts between the two lives, which it connects. It was the third of
March 1887, three months before I was seven years old.

On the afternoon of that eventful day, I stood on the porch, dumb, expectant. I guessed vaguely from my mother's signs and from the hurrying to and fro in the house that something unusual was about to happen, so I went to the door and waited on the steps. The afternoon sun penetrated the mass of honeysuckle that covered the porch, and fell on my upturned face. My fingers lingered almost unconsciously on the familiar leaves and blossoms, which had just come forth to greet the sweet southern spring. I did not know what the future held of marvel or surprise for me. Anger and bitterness had preyed upon me continually for weeks and a deep languor had succeeded this passionate struggle.

Have you ever been at sea in a dense fog, when it seemed as if a tangible white darkness shut you in, and the great ship, tense and anxious, groped her way toward the shore with plummet and sounding line, and you waited with beating heart for something to happen? I was like that ship before my education began, only I was without compass or sounding line, and had no way of knowing how near the harbour was. "Light! Give me light!" was the wordless cry of my soul, and the light of love shone on me in that very hour.

I felt approaching footsteps, I stretched out my hand as I supposed to my mother. Some one took it, and I was caught up and held close in the arms of her who had come to reveal all things to me, and, more than all things else, to love me.

The morning after my teacher came she led me into her room and gave me a doll. The little blind children at the Perkins Institution had sent it and Laura Bridgman had dressed it; but I did not know this until afterward. When I had played with it a little while, Miss Sullivan slowly spelled into my hand the word "d-o-l-l." I was at once interested in this finger play and tried to imitate it. When I finally succeeded in making the letters correctly I was flushed with childish pleasure and pride. Running downstairs to my mother I held up my hand and made the letters for doll. I did not know that I was spelling a word or even that words existed; I was simply making my fingers go in monkey-like imitation. In the days that followed I learned to spell in this uncomprehending way a great many words, among them pin, hat, cup and a few verbs like sit, stand and walk. But my teacher had been with me several weeks before I understood that everything has a name.

One day, while I was playing with my new doll, Miss Sullivan put my big rag doll into my lap also, spelled "d-o-l-l" and tried to make me understand that "d-o-l-l" applied to both. Earlier in the day we had had a tussle over the words "m-u-g" and "w-a-t-e-r." Miss Sullivan had tried to impress it upon me that "m-u-g" is mug and that "w-a-t-e-r" is water, but I persisted in confounding the two. In despair she had dropped the subject for the time, only to renew it at the first opportunity. I became impatient at her repeated attempts and, seizing the new doll, I dashed it upon the
floor. I was keenly delighted when I felt the fragments of the broken doll at my feet. Neither sorrow nor regret followed my passionate outburst. I had not loved the doll. In the still, dark world in which I lived there was no strong sentiment or tenderness. I felt my teacher sweep the fragments to one side of the hearth, and I had a sense of satisfaction that the cause of my discomfort was removed. She brought me my hat, and I knew I was going out into the warm sunshine. This thought, if a wordless sensation may be called a thought, made me hop and skip with pleasure.

We walked down the path to the well-house, attracted by the fragrance of the honeysuckle with which it was covered. Some one was drawing water and my teacher placed my hand under the spout. As the cool stream gushed over one hand she spelled into the other the word water, first slowly, then rapidly. I stood still, my whole attention fixed upon the motions of her fingers. Suddenly I felt a misty consciousness as of something
forgotten—a thrill of returning thought; and somehow the mystery of language was revealed to me. I knew then that "w-a-t-e r"
meant the wonderful cool something that was flowing over my hand. That living word awakened my soul, gave it light, hope, joy, set it free! There were barriers still, it is true, but barriers that could in time be swept away.

I left the well-house eager to learn. Everything had a name, and each name gave birth to a new thought. As we returned to the house every object which I touched seemed to quiver with life. That was because

I saw everything with the strange, new sight that had come to me. On entering the door I remembered the doll I had broken. I felt my way to the hearth and picked up the pieces.
I tried vainly to put them together. Then my eyes filled with tears; for I realized what I had done, and for the first time I felt repentance and sorrow.

I learned a great many new words that day. I do not remember what they all were; but I do know that mother, father, sister, teacher were among them—words that were to make the world blossom for me, "like Aaron's rod, with flowers." It would have been difficult to find a happier child than I was as I lay in my crib
at the close of that eventful day and lived over the joys it had brought me, and for the first time longed for a new day to come.

NOTICE: *To the best of this writer's knowledge, Keller's essay is copyright free and is in Public Domain.*

CONSIDER THE FOLLOWING

How to Write a Narrative Essay

Start by drafting an effective thesis statement that will display both the topic and a preview of what is to be told. Here is an example of an effective thesis statement:

- ***The day of my final exam was a tragedy***.

In this thesis statement, the topic of the story I am about to tell is ***the day of my final exam***; the tone I will use for this essay is a ***tragic* tone**. These details are what I will develop in the body of my essay. You'll see how I do this in the example essay below.

Once you have written your thesis statement, stick to a point of view. You should remain steady throughout your writing. Write only the noteworthy details that are relevant to the event or events. Be as descriptive in your choice of words as you can. Vibrant details make a narrative essay motivating.

When you write these brilliant details, however, try to avoid wordiness and flowery expressions. Too many words or details can confuse the heart of your essay and also confuse the reader.

Remember to use your outline and the details you listed that support your thesis statement. These will help point you and your paper to the right direction.

CONSIDER THE FOLLOWING

Narrative Essay Example

Here is another essay written by one of my college students:

Throughout my life, I have experienced many eventful days; some events were more pleasant than others were. However, one of the most unforgettable was the day of my final exam for my writing class last semester. That day was a tragedy.

It all started when I woke up one and half hours later than I had planned. The night before the exam day, I had set my old radio alarm to go off at 6:00 in the morning. When I opened my eyes, I looked at the clock in disbelief; it was 7:35. I got up in a panic as I realized that I had less than an hour to get ready and go to school. The time of the exam was 8:30. Ignoring my morning rituals of drinking a cup of coffee and taking a shower, I put some clothes on and rushed out my door.

Then, to make matters worse, my car refused to start. As I turned the key in the ignition, all I could hear was click, click, and click. After several attempts, I realized that my car battery had died, so I hurriedly called my road service company. The 20 minutes I waited for help seemed a lot longer. Finally, help arrived, and I was able to start the car. In great anxiety, I zoomed off, hoping to reach my school in 20 minutes.

Midway to school, and just as I was calming myself, I saw flashing red lights in my rearview mirror. For a moment, I could not believe what was happening, but it was true; I was pulled over by a police officer. I tried in vain to explain my dilemma, but she did not seem to care and issued me a speeding ticket. It was now 8:50, and the writing exam had started. Fortunately, my instructor allowed me to take the exam.

I had to write an essay in 30 minutes. I collected my thoughts, tried to relax and relieve myself from anxiety, and wrote. I was later happily surprised to find out that I had written a good essay and passed the class. Although that morning was a tragedy that I will never forget, I realized that all the writing practice I had been doing helped me.

You can see that this essay is **about a personal experience** that the writer had. She used the first-person pronoun (I), and this story certainly did not require any research. What usually makes a narrative essay good is that the writer uses personal experience.

That experience can happen a number of ways: reading a book, visiting a museum, or getting pulled over by the police for speeding. On the other hand, a writer can create a narrative through conducting research into a topic and reporting on it. In this case, the writer does not need to use the first-person pronoun.

The Great Writer of Inspiration: Helen Keller

CONSIDER THE FOLLOWING

The Explanatory Essay

The function of the explanatory essay is to clarify or to familiarize your reader with your information. Most often, the subject of an explanatory essay will be something that you and your reader are familiar with.

This type of essay is required in most colleges. The essay styles that are most often used with this essay category are *definition, example, process, and analysis*. With all of these styles, the goal is to provide information about a topic.

How to Write an Explanatory Essay

Explanatory essays are a conventional, more so than descriptive and narrative essays. The topics covered in these essays are significant and academic.

When you begin an explanatory essay, you must have a particular event, topic, or consequence that you are going to discuss. Brainstorming, creating a thesis statement, and developing an outline are just the same as in any other essay. However, these types of essays may require some research and fact-checking/

On the other hand, you can also use an explanatory essay to write about topics that may not require fact checking or research.

In order to use a topic for an explanatory essay, the writer ought to perform some research in order to use accurate information. These essays almost always entail some kind of research.

Also, an explanatory essay almost always talks about some sort of process or procedure. To deliver explanation about a subject or topic is a key part of an explanatory essay.

Compare and Contrast Essays

To create an effective essay using this style, it is important that writers use appropriate facts and details. When a writer wants to influence the reader of a point of view, she or he should be sure to include the particulars that reinforce and highlight the written opinion.

In general, you should absolutely brainstorm and cluster your ideas with this essay style. It is very valuable to help you see all the facts and details grouped together. This will help you choose the precise details to make connections that clearly show similarities and differences.

Also, using transitional words and phrases will assist you produce a united and coherent essay. Sometimes called **cohesive devices**, transitional words and phrases prepare your readers to appreciate what you're going to explain to them. They recognize that something important is about to be said and lead or cue the reader from point to point in a clear, comprehensible way.

For compare and contrast essays, words such as *like*, *similar to*, *also*, *unlike*, and *on the other hand* make it clear to your readers when you are comparing or contrasting. *Like*, *similar to*, and *also* demonstrate similarities (comparing), while *unlike* and *on the other hand* show differences (contrasting).

Here are some examples of how to use cue words to introduce ideas that are being compared and contrasted:

- *Similar to my French teacher, my Italian teacher was in his early 30*
- *Both San Jose City College and Santa Ana College are similar in these areas.*
- *Unlike my French teacher, my Italian teacher was much more relaxed.*

While the majority of the student population at San Jose City College is over the age of 25, the majority at Santa Ana College is under the age of 25.

How to Begin Your Compare and Contrast Essay

First, you begin by deciding what your focus will be. A unique quality of a compare and contrast essay is that you must select two topics and that these two topics must be comparable. For instance, you can select two countries, but you cannot create a logical compare and contrast essay if you picked a country and a planet!

Once you decide on the topics you will write about, next comes the thesis statement. How you write your thesis statement will set the tone for the entire essay. The thesis statement for a compare and contrast essay can be long. So, it is acceptable if it is more than one sentence. For instance:

Although my teachers were European males, and about they were about the same age, the differences between them were striking. They were clearly different in their personalities, teaching methods, and relationships with students.

You must be very clear about what elements you are comparing and contrasting, and you must be sure that any conclusions you make will be based on your supporting details. So, gathering and organizing your supporting details will be very important.

You must make sure they are correct; this may involve thorough research and citing of your sources. Also, your details must logically support the topic sentence of the paragraph and the thesis statement. Here you will need to use the brainstorming and clustering techniques we discussed earlier.

When you have your thesis statement and finish brainstorming and clustering, it is time to develop an outline to guide you through the writing process. You can use a couple of organizational patterns for your outline. In the next chapter, I will describe the *block organizational method*. Then, in Chapter 4, we will examine the *item-by-item organizational method*.

To decide which of these two methods to use, consider the nature of the topic and your readers. If the topic has a lot of detail, the block method would probably be better because it allows you to group the details of each topic. However, when you have a more limited amount of information, then I recommend you use the item-by-item method. This one can work easily with our five-paragraph essay pattern, because you can pick the number of items to compare and contrast.

During the development stage of the essay, I recommend that you go back and ensure that each paragraph has a clear topic sentence and plenty of logical supporting details. Also, make sure that all your paragraphs create a united and cohesive essay.

What do you think now? Does this seem doable? As I mentioned earlier, once you know the trick, you will be able to write effectively.

CONSIDER THE FOLLOWING

The Block Organizational Method

In the block organizational method or format, you will talk about each subject's characteristics in its own paragraph. So you will say what your first subject is like in one paragraph; then you will say what your second subject is like in the next paragraph. This will give you an overall picture of how one subject is similar to and different from the other. Just think of this style as creating blocks of information for each item.

Let us take a look at what a complete essay based on this topic might look like.

Block Format Essay Example

"I will always remember the instructors who taught me to speak and read French and Italian. Although my teachers were European males and are about the same age, the differences between them were striking. They were clearly different in their personalities, teaching methods, and relationships with students.

My French teacher was a young Frenchman in his late 20s or early 30s. He had just come to the United States from Paris, and his personality reflected the Parisian culture. He was serious and took the French language seriously. He was also formal, always wearing a suit and a tie. Although he would smile at our comments and jokes, he would soon return to being serious. His teaching methods were orthodox: He would ask the class to read French texts aloud and follow that with questions and discussions. His quizzes and exams were hard, testing us on both oral and written language.

All the students felt that he was unapproachable and were reluctant to ask questions. Although at the time I thought I did not like him, later felt lucky to have had him as my French teacher. I now speak and understand French well, thanks to him.

Like my French teacher, my Italian teacher was also young, probably in his early 30s. However, he had been in the United States longer than my French teacher had and was much more relaxed. He would always come to class in jeans and T-shirts; I never saw him wear a suit. He was certainly unorthodox in his teaching methods: He would speak in Italian throughout the class time whether we understood him or not. He would respond to our questions, which we would ask in English, in Italian. His quizzes and exams were easy, and the whole class did well. He was very friendly with the students, and we all felt as though he was a friend rather than a teacher. His teaching methods must have been effective, because the whole class felt comfortable with the Italian language by the time the semester ended.

It is interesting for me now to remember these two language teachers. While they were both from two neighboring European countries, their cultures were distinctly different. Though they were about the same age, their personalities, which were reflected in their style of dress and relationships with students, were far apart. Even though they were both teaching languages, their methods were not the same. Yet they both succeeded in their efforts.

I had these teachers more than 10 years ago, yet I vividly remember them. Seldom have we met people who influence our lives; it is even less often to keep memories of them. However, some teachers have the ability to leave such an impact that we will always remember them. My French and Italian teachers were such persons."

As you can see, the fourth paragraph is where the essay focuses on the similarities and differences that are described in the second and the third paragraphs. Basically, this is where the comparing and contrasting takes place.

Now let us move on and take a look at the second organizational structure—*item-by-item*.

CONSIDER THE FOLLOWING

Item-by-Item Organizational Method

Another method for writing a compare and contrast essay is the item-by-item method. This method can be a bit more demanding. The topic of each body paragraph is based on a single characteristic of the two topics you are comparing and contrasting in your essay. The supporting details in each paragraph will then explain both the similarities and the differences between the two topics.

You need to cautiously organize the information in your body paragraphs. Whether or not you begin with similarities or differences, you should put the information in the same order for each paragraph. Sometimes you may have more differences than similarities. But regardless of what the topic for the paragraph is or how many similarities or differences there are; I always start each paragraph with the same type of information.

Okay, let us move on and see how to do it. Here is a sample item-by-item outline for an essay that is comparing and contrasting San Jose City College and Santa Ana College.

Below is an example of the complete essay for this outline. I want you to note how the body paragraphs are organized. Specifically, look at each topic sentence and the order of the supporting details.

CONSIDER THE FOLLOWING

Item-by-Item Example:

"Most community colleges in California are fairly similar in what they do and whom they serve, though each will have some unique characteristics, San Jose Community College and Santa Ana College share similarities in their student population, special services, and teaching staff. However, these two schools have some significant differences in these areas too.

San Jose Community College (SJCC) has a student population of about 10,000, and a large percentage of these students are Asian. Additionally, most students at SJCC are over age 25 and work while attending school. Reports also show that a vast majority of students are non-native English speakers. Finally, the majority of students are interested in the humanities as their area of study. Similarly, Santa Ana College (SAC) has a student population of about 10,000, most of whom are Asian. However, unlike SJCC, most students at SAC are under 25 and do not work while attending school. Contrary to SJCC, at SAC the vast majority of students are native speakers, and most are interested in science as their area of study.

Both colleges offer similar special services to their students. SJCC offers financial aid and health services, as well as transportation services to disabled students. In addition, SJCC provides lab assistance and tutoring. Similarly, SAC offers financial aid and health services to their students. However, unlike SJCC, SAC does not offer transportation services to disabled students. While SAC also provides lab assistance and tutoring, their program is not as widely used as it is at SJCC.

The teaching staff at SJCC is highly qualified and experienced. They are always ready to help students and work on promoting student success. Teachers at SJCC tend to be older and more traditional in their teaching methods. At SAC, the teachers are similarly qualified and experienced. They are equally ready to help students and promote student success. Unlike SJCC, teachers at SAC are younger and more progressive in their teaching methods.

SJCC and SAC share a number of similarities in certain areas. However, they also have some key differences. These differences do not necessarily distinguish one school above the other. They are both equally successful accredited institutions that have much to offer students."

Did you note how the three supporting paragraphs described each of the specific items I wrote about in the thesis statement? Each paragraph began with a topic sentence about its subject (student population, special services, and teaching staff). Then, when the discussion began, I always started with the information about San Jose Community College and finished with Santa Ana College. First came the similarities, and then came any differences.

Following a consistent pattern will help you communicate your ideas to the readers in a clear, specific, and successful manner.

CONSIDER THE FOLLOWING

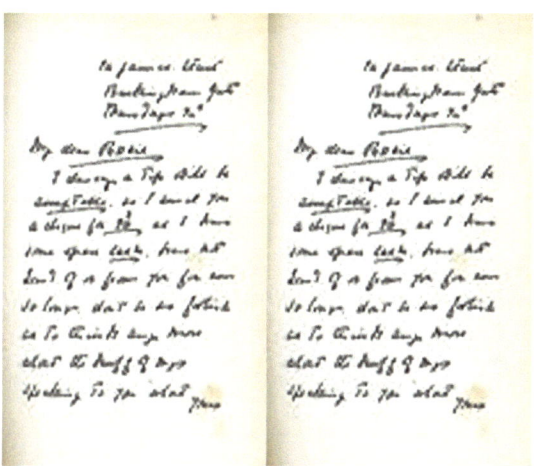

The good news is that most essays, whether college essays or standard exam essays, do not ask writers to write on both. The essay question will often be compare or contrast, but not compare and contrast. Only in college, you might have to write a long paper on both, specifically if the question deals with literature.

Again, always remember that when you compare, you look at similarities between the two items, ideas, or matters. When you contrast, you look at the differences.

Another note of significance, even though at times you will need to write essays in which you specifically compare or contrast two ideas, people, places, or items, you will find it necessary other times to integrate this pattern in other forms and types of writings as well.

On this note, here is an excellent quote on learning by the master Alexandre Dumas. He wrote:

"Learning does not make one learned: there are those who have knowledge and those who have understanding. The first requires memory and the second philosophy"

"Le Comte de Monte-Cristo" by Alexandre Dumas

Cause and Effect Essays

We may remember that it is important for any writer, as well as for critical readers, to know the general categories and styles of writing. Each type of writing has its own format, organization, and technique. Although we may find an essay written as descriptive, narrative, or explanatory, it is not uncommon to find that many essays combine several styles in one.

This makes *cause and effect* essays of utmost significance. Not only that we may need to use cause and effect in other essay modes, but unlike descriptive and narrative essays, in cause and effect we have to make extra effort to pay attention to facts and to our sources. Also, the information we may use in this essay style must validate a logical and correct relationship between the cause and the effect.

A cause and effect essay can be written in one of two ways. First, you can look at a single cause and discuss the multiple effects that resulted from it. Second, you can use a single effect and examine multiple causes for it. To say it simply, a cause and effect essay looks at what causes what to happen or what the consequences are of something happening

When you write a cause and effect essay, you must answer two important questions:

Why did something happen? (The cause)

What happened because of this? (The effect)

For example, let us say that we want to look at the reasons why people immigrate to the United States. This means that we are focusing the essay on a single effect (people immigrating to the United States) and looking for multiple causes for why it happens. Here is how you might begin organizing your thoughts:

Effect: *People immigrating to the United States*

- Cause 1: Economic reasons
- Cause 2: Political reasons
- Cause 3: Personal reasons

Using this information, you can create a single-sentence thesis statement that explains the relationship you described above. Here is the thesis statement:

> *Some people choose to immigrate to the United States for economic, political, and personal reasons.*

On the other hand, we may want to focus an essay on a single cause (for example, increase in lung cancer) and look at what effects happened because of it. Here are some topics that I came up with while brainstorming:

Cause: *An increased number of teenage female smokers since 1985.*

- Effect 1: More cases of emphysema in women over 30.
- Effect 2: Higher taxes due to cigarette-related health-care costs of women at or below the poverty level.

- Effect 3: Triple the number of the cases of childhood asthma due to secondhand smoke.

With our thesis statement, then, we will have to show that we are developing an essay on the effects of having more women begin smoking since 1985. Our thesis statement might be something like this:

> *The increased number of women smokers since 1985 has contributed to many negative trends in health, taxes, and childhood asthma.*

When we write cause and effect essays, it is very important to be cautious about logical relationship between the ideas we discuss. We work on ensuring that there is a direct relationship between the cause and the effect. This is a significant point, especially for writers whose native language is not English.

A Note on Culture:

Many cultures see the relationship between cause and effect a little differently. They might believe that all things relate, as it is the case in Arabic culture. Thus, a writer from such culture who writes in English might state a cause and effect relationship that would not be considered by English readers as logical or coherent.

Now, let us look at another example in more detail.

CONSIDER THE FOLLOWING

Single Cause, Multiple Effects

Try to assume that you are asked to respond to the following essay topic:

Discuss the possible effects of dropping out of high school.

Can you pick out the cause? That is right, the cause is *dropping out of high school*. So, your job is to find the *effects* that dropping out of high school might have on a young person.

To respond to an essay topic like that, what is the best way to create a thesis statement? Take a moment and write down some ideas. When you are finished, continue reading and see how I developed my thesis statement.

"Dropping out of high school, which is a nation-wide problem, is destructive in many ways: It limits one's likelihoods of getting a suitable job; it forces one to live in poverty; and it reduces one's ability to deal with everyday problems in life."

I wrote this thesis statement so that it controlled the essay. A thesis statement, as you recall, is a sentence that includes the controlling idea of the essay. Remember that it must not be too broad, too narrow, an announcement, and, of course, it must be a complete sentence. My thesis statement shows what the essay is about (effects of dropping out of high school) and how the information is organized (the three negative effects).

From this point, I structured my essay so that each effect would have its own paragraph. These three body paragraphs, you will remember, are *supporting paragraphs*. Each supporting paragraph will start with a topic sentence. Following the topic sentence, I will use specific details that support the topic sentence. Some examples of these details are anecdotes, statistics, and anything else that will help develop the topic sentence.

Now I will talk about the other example of a cause and effect essay: when you focus on a single effect and look for multiple causes.

Single Effect, Multiple Causes

In the same manner, we might have to write an essay that focuses on the *effect* rather than the causes. Here is another essay question for you to consider:

> *Why do many young people drop out of high school?*

You can see this is almost exactly the same question as the example above. However, the question is asking about a single effect or result (young people dropping out of school) and asking us to find the causes for it. For this essay, I would use the following causes: *low self-esteem due to rejection from friends; an undiagnosed learning disability; and a negative home life that does not value education.*

Before we move on, I want to share some important information about this specific essay style. To effectively use the cause and effect style, one must know about the transitional words and phrases that apply to it. Sometimes in cause and effect essays, it is difficult for readers to follow the logic of the writer from one point to the next. Also, readers may not see the relationships between ideas in the same paragraph or between paragraphs. This is when using transitional words and phrases will help.

First, let me provide a list of the most common transitional words and phrases.

For *causes*:	For Effect:
- Another is - Because - Due to - First - For - For this reason - One cause is - Second - Since	- Another is - As a result - Consequently - Hence - One result is - Resulted in - So - Then - Therefore - Thus

Below are some examples of how to use transitional words and phrases. These three paragraphs are based on the three causes I listed for why young people drop out of school. (Note that the transitional words and phrases are in bold.)

One reason why some students drop out of school is their helplessness in dealing with the school environment. Life in high schools can be socially challenging for some students. Adolescents seek love and acceptance from their peers, and if they do not feel accepted, they develop low self-esteem. ***As a result*** of their low self-esteem, they make the hasty decision to drop out of school.

Low self-esteem is not the only possible reason for

dropping out of school; having a learning disability *is another*. Many children suffer from some form of a learning disability that is not detected. **Because of this**, some students might feel inept in dealing with academic challenges. **Hence**, they decide to leave school.

In addition to their self-esteem problems and their possible undiagnosed learning disability, some students might be living in a negative home environment that does not value education. **Consequently**, they do not receive much-needed support. **For this reason,** they find themselves unable to handle school; thus, they drop out.

Now that we have a wide-ranging understanding of how cause and effect essays are developed, we will examine both the causal analysis and the effect analysis separately in order to clarify both the process and the techniques.

Writer William Somerset

Causal Analysis

As we learned above, causal analysis essays are essays that focus on what causes what to happen. When we address and analyze causes, we are trying to understand the relationship of events that resulted in a particular outcome. We actually do this in everyday life; when a situation or a problem arises, we try to discover the cause or causes for the situation or the problem.

When we try to understand the cause of something, we may find that many causes contributed to bringing about the outcome. Take, for example, the devastating disease cancer. It is hardly logical to assume that cancer is brought about by one cause; there must be several contributing factors at work.

So, in general terms, when we write a causal analysis essay, we often list more than one cause. We take each cause and show how it contributes to bringing about the result we are addressing.

Read the following two paragraphs a student has written to explain the reasons why she wanted to be a math teacher:

One reason why I wanted to become a math teacher was my previous success in math. During high school, I was always at the top of my class. In fact, I got high scores in this subject because I developed a special skill solving any kind of math problem easily; my teachers recognized my strong skills and my ability to think mathematically.

That recognition encouraged me to choose math as my major and to aspire to become a math teacher.

Another reason why I chose to teach math was my desire to compete with male candidates who wanted to become math teachers. At that time in my country, few women were admitted into the study of math because it was considered a male career. I wanted to demonstrate to my parents, to my teachers, and above all, to myself that I could reach my goal, which was to be a successful math teacher. Therefore, as soon as I could, I enrolled at a university, studied for five years, and received my bachelor's degree in mathematics as well as math teaching credentials.

Notice that the two reasons above are independent of each other, yet they both contributed to why the writer wanted to become a math teacher. This detail brings me to an important rule to remember when you are working on the causal analysis of a cause and effect essay:

Rule to Consider

You must list your causes in a certain order based on the type of cause. If the causes *are not* related to each other but are related to the effect, you can arrange the order of the paragraphs any way you like.

Here is an example a student has written on the reasons why she decided to take one of my advanced writing classes:

"There are many reasons why I decided to take an advanced writing class. One reason was to improve my reading and writing skills. A second reason was to meet people who had similar interests to mine. A third reason was to prepare myself for graduate school.

My decision to enroll in a writing class was driven by my interest in improving my reading and writing skills. Although overall I considered myself a good writer, I knew that there was much to learn. I needed to learn how to write academic papers, which are often required by professors. I knew that taking a writing class would give me an exposure to academic writings, and I knew I would have an opportunity to practice writing such papers.

Another reason why I decided to take an advanced writing class was to meet people whose interests were similar to my interests. I am interested in going to graduate school, and I hoped to find classmates who would also want to go to graduate school. I thought that meeting such people would encourage me and provide me some support.

My interest in improving my writing skills and in meeting people were not the only reasons why I registered for a writing class; I also wanted to prepare myself academically to succeed in graduate school. Graduate schools are demanding and require a lot of reading and writing; I thought that by taking an advanced writing class, I would develop better skills that would help me succeed."

If the causes *are* related to each other, you must arrange them in order of importance. In this case, always start with the most important cause as it relates to the effect.

Here is another example a student has written on the reasons why she decided to take an advanced writing class. Notice that the writer lists *developing interest in reading* as a reason that resulted in another reason *enhancing vocabulary power and communication skills*. This logical sequence is very important to watch for.

"Besides wanting an opportunity to find myself as a writer, one reason that made me enroll in a writing class was to develop an interest in reading. Thanks to my writing teacher, I started to read magazines such as *Newsweek*, the newspaper, and novels. Before, in my spare time, I used to watch television or movies. Now, I enjoy better a piece of reading from a book or even my own written essays. I learned that a good way to learn how to improve my thinking and my communication skills was through reading. Moreover, reading has become a routine in my life.

Developing interest in reading enhanced my vocabulary power and, thus, my communication skills. So, another reason why I decided to take a writing class was to enhance the effectiveness of my communication skills by learning new vocabulary. When I needed to speak in English, I always had the same problem. I had to use the same words I knew repeatedly. I wanted to be able to maintain deep conversations with my customers at the restaurant where I work. As a waitress, I am supposed to give excellent customer service, and my new vocabulary helps me communicate more effectively."

Effect Analysis

You already know that to identify if something is an effect, it must be something that happened as a result of a specific cause. When you research and analyze the effects of something, you are trying to understand the relationship of the effect to the cause. You can approach this analysis the same way you approached the causal analysis.

Below are some different sets of causes and effects. See if you can think of some effects that might be the result of these causes.

Cause	Effect
Getting a college degree	• Getting a good job • Ability to advance at work • Making more money • Ability to confront and solve problems
Getting a speeding ticket	• Large fine • Increased cost of insurance • Loss of income • Loss of driver license
Investing in the stock market	• Earning a lot of money quickly • Losing a lot of money quickly • Spending too much time on the computer

Here is an essay a student has written on the effects of going to college:

"Education helps us have a better and enjoyable life. It opens our eyes and minds and helps us look at and understand the world and people differently. It shapes our lives and personalities, so we cannot survive without it. It really makes our lives more easy and pleasant. Attending college enhances knowledge; it helps us acquire better jobs with high salaries; and, most important, it helps us develop strong communication skills.

Among the effects attending college will have on a person is enhancing knowledge. Colleges provide learners with knowledge of advanced technology and science. Today, many companies carefully select their employees based on their skills, training, and knowledge. Thus, only those employees who have the required skills and knowledge are the eligible candidates. Being knowledgeable and moving along with technology are necessary to survive in today's highly competitive market. For example, my husband, after graduating with an M.S. degree in electronic engineering, was hired by a high-tech telecommunication company in 1992. He is still working in the same company because he is maintaining and updating his working knowledge by taking advanced courses in college.

Another effect is that college graduates acquire better jobs with high salaries. With a college degree, people will be able to have high-paying jobs, so they earn more money than high school graduates do. High-salary positions require higher education. The higher education people get after high school increases the chances that they will earn good pay. If people make more money, they will have a more comfortable and an easier life by purchasing new and beautiful houses and luxury cars. They can send their children to the best schools and universities and secure their futures. When people make more money, they may have more savings deposited for their retirement and rainy days. I still remember my father's advice: Get more education to make more money. Now I believe he is right, because money accelerates our success in life.

Additionally, a crucial effect of attending college is developing strong communication skills. Education beyond the high school level gives people many benefits, including meeting new people and exploring their interests. It helps them communicate with people who have different cultures and backgrounds. Our ancestors used to live in closed societies, but we don't. We go to college to set up our personal growth and friendship, improve and extend our social activities, meet new friends, and share our experiences. For example, I don't feel that I am alone, because I have made some new and good friends with different ethnicities and cultures in San Jose City College by taking the ESL courses.

In short, going to college brings about many positive results. The effects of going to college play an important role in people's lives by making a bridge between them and the world. Going to college helps people improve their lives in many ways."

Did you see how this writer laid out all the effects that the single cause (attending college) had? The examples used in the essay were vivid and clear. As a reader, I could plainly understand the relationship this writer was explaining between going to college and all the effects that came from that single cause.

We took an in-depth look at cause and effect essays. Once you master the elements of this essay, it will be a powerful communication tool for you. You learned how to focus on finding and examining the effects of a certain cause. From this you discovered how to address and analyze causes and how to understand the relationship of events that result from a particular outcome.

Making connections and understanding the relationship of causes and effects is something we do in everyday life, hopefully, in a logical manner – although that is not always the case. So now I hope that you can apply this skill when you are asked to write an essay at school or a memo or a business report at the workplace. Also, remember your audience! When writing for English speakers, write about relationships that are based on tangible facts that the reader can clearly see and understand. Doing so will help you create strong and successful essays.

The most significant aspect of this part of learning is creating logical relationships between elements. Creating an effective thesis statement that clearly demonstrates this relationship is a key part of any cause and effect essay. Now that you know the secrets to success, I know you will do well.

CONSIDER THE FOLLOWING 181

True Hero: Martin Luther King

The Argumentation Essay

When we write or make an argument, our rationale is to take a position on an issue, reinforce it by providing one or more reasons, and get others to accept it. Arguments require reasoning. We make a proclamation, which is the main idea of the argument, and we deliver facts and illustrations to support this assertion. Does this make sense?

Unlike what many believe, the purpose for writing argumentation essays is not always to persuade readers to do one thing or another. Although we will sometimes have to use arguments to persuade readers, not all arguments are for persuasion. Persuasion is a different matter.

For example, when someone tries to convince us to believe in something, to buy something, or to follow a particular rule, this is persuasion. Political and religious speeches are good examples of persuasive style. Advertisements that we, sadly, watch on television, hear on the radio, or read in newspapers and magazines are also designed, very poorly I must add, to persuade us to do or buy something. Sometimes, some writers who try to persuade readers fail to follow logic and commit outrageous fallacies.

An argument, on the other hand, is an attempt to prove, establish, or support an assertion or a claim. In essence, an argument essay has a thesis statement and a premise or premises to support an assertion. A *premise* is a statement that is assumed to be true and from which a conclusion can be drawn.

In argumentation writing, then, we take a position on a debatable issue and defend that position. This could be a political issue, a religious matter, or any issue that people feel strongly about. For example, consider these debatable questions:

- Should smoking be banned in all public places?
- Should we restrict gun ownership?
- Should communities make breed-specific laws against owning certain types of dogs?

These are called *controversial topics*, which means that people often strongly agree or disagree. But which side is right? That is for each person to decide. However, when we write an argumentation essay, we try to influence people to believe what we believe.

Our goals in argumentation writing are (1) to defend a particular point of view and (2) to change the way readers think about an issue.

If the purpose is to persuade, then we also want (3) to convince readers to take an action they might not otherwise be disposed to take. These are three very difficult tasks to do. However, to convince readers to follow our way of thinking or at least understand our point of view, we need to build arguments that are sound and logical enough to stand up to our opponents' arguments.

CONSIDER THE FOLLOWING

Organizing an Argumentation Essay

If we need to write an essay on a controversial issue, we will have to do some serious and logical brainstorming. This is where we will begin to develop the logic and details of our contention. We ought to first ask ourselves some questions like these:

- What do some people think about this issue?
- Why do they think that way?
- What are their arguments?
- How do they support their arguments?

Then think about our own assessments on the issue, and ask ourselves the same questions.

Once we have completed this brainstorming stage, we develop an outline to help guide us when writing. The outline is exactly the same outline you learned earlier except we focus on the reasons for the statement we made in our thesis statement:

It will look something like this:

I. Introduction
    - Introduce the topic
    - Thesis statement with
    - Reason One
    - Reason Two
    - Reason Three

II. Reason One
    - Topic Sentence
    - Support
    - Detail
    - Detail
    - Detail

Then we do then same for reason two and reason three; then we add the conclusion, which wraps up our ideas in a very coherent and strong voice.

As I explained earlier, of all the essay styles, argumentation is the most complex. In argumentation, we are not only making an assertion but also explaining how we came to make such an assertion. This is not always easy to do unless we have a clear understanding of the basic principles of critical (logical) thinking and how to apply them.

Logical vs. Fallacious Thinking

Critical thinking will help you build a strong, logical, and defensible argument, while fallacious thinking will cobble together a wobbly, irrational, easily refuted argument. Which choice is better seems obvious, but one would be surprised at how many people unwittingly fall for fallacies.

Analytical Thinking

In order to develop a reliable argument, one that is effective and factual, we need good critical-thinking skills. These skills help us impartially inspect what we see, hear, or read to conclude whether the claims made are dependable, logical, and rational.

When we think critically, we do not take things at face value, believing everything we are told. Instead, we sensibly consider the information, separating it from the distortions of the speaker's impressions, interpretations, and prejudgments—as well as our own.

How do we apply critical or logical thinking to writing an argumentation essay? For one thing, we ask the following questions:

- Is the topic truly debatable, which means if there are at least two sides to it?
- Is it based on sound logic, or are we arguing from emotions?
- How are we reaching the conclusions we are proclaiming? In other words, are the premises true and logical, and do they lead to reasonable conclusions?

It is often helpful to work backward from our premises, which are the building blocks of the overall argument. Let me give an example, first of illogical thinking based on faulty premises.

Illogical Thinking

- Premise 1: People who wear glasses are smart.
- Premise 2: Jane wears glasses.
- Conclusion: Therefore, Juan is smart.

The first premise, "People who wear glasses are smart," is faulty because glasses are for eyesight, not intelligence. It is not a true or logical statement. The premise, remember, needs to be true in all cases.

This next example shows logical thinking based on sound premises.

Logical Thinking

- Premise 1: Cats have whiskers.
- Premise 2: Fred is a cat.
- Conclusion: Therefore, Fred has whiskers.

"Cats have whiskers" is a sound premise because it is true that all cats have whiskers. Of course some may not have whiskers, but that would be a health matter and not the norm.

Now let us identify what some common fallacies are so that not only we protect ourselves from commercial predators, but also we can avoid putting them in our own writing.

Identifying Fallacies

While critical thinking will help build a strong, sound argument, fallacies can cause problems and create a weak foundation for arguments. Fallacies are invalid or false premises or wrongly reached conclusions. If the reasons we provide do not support the conclusion we reach, the argument is fallacious. There are many types of fallacies, yet they all have *the same principle*: *the conclusion is illogical*.

We will examine three of the most common fallacies found in writing: either-or, lack-of-proof, and emotional fallacies. Now, we really do not need to know the name of each fallacy; however, we need to be able to discover that a conclusion is fallacious. When we can identify fallacies in an argument, it will protect us from deceitful messages in advertising and help us write solid, reliable, valid, and effective arguments.

CONSIDER THE FOLLOWING

1. Either-Or Fallacies

What do you think of this statement?

You either hate television, or you are not intelligent.

The operative word here is or—it falsely limits one's options to two. This limiting of options is illogical because many intelligent people like television. Thus, the argument is invalid. This either-or fallacy is commonly used, so be sure you avoid it when writing.

2. Lack-of-Proof Fallacies

Here is another statement to consider:

If you cannot prove that animals think, then they do not.

Such an argument illogically assumes that since you cannot prove something true, it is therefore false. Unfortunately, this is also a very common fallacy that many writers include in their argument essays. However, you should always remember that *lack of proof is not proof.*

3. Emotional Fallacies

Another common fallacy, often used by the media and some corporations, is designed to influence someone's judgment by appealing to his or her emotions. Emotional fallacies focus on a person's pity, respect for authority, and fear of negative consequences. For example, evaluate these arguments:

- You must use Fresh Breath toothpaste, or else no one will like you.
- This must be a good product, because Opera uses it.
- If you have a heart, you would send money to the needy.

These statements base the argument on emotions and thus, lack reason and logic. They threaten shame, and try to make people afraid so that they will not think for themselves. When people in power want to influence others, they use these kinds of fallacious arguments to get people to do things they otherwise would not do.

It might be a good idea for you to pay attention the next time you hear or read something like that and try to identify it. It is fun.

When I worked as a journalist, one of my hobbies was to invite salespeople and religious preachers who came to my door to enter my apartment and talk to me about what they were selling or doing. I used to listen carefully to their words and observe their techniques in trying to persuade me to buy what they were selling or to subscribe to their faith. They did not know, of course, that I was examining them and their logic. It was an excellent mental exercise for me from which I learned a lot.

You hear and read so many illogical arguments every day. It is wise to develop a skill that will help you identify what is a reasonable, reliable, and valid argument. This will protect you from those who want to persuade you to do things you do not want to do.

It is equally your responsibility as writers to avoid making arguments that are not solid and logical. In writing, the writer is the only source of information; the readers are not present to argue. Therefore, it is the writer's responsibility to be clear, concise, logical, reasonable, and truthful.

Now that we have a solid foundation for thinking critically and avoiding fallacies, let us learn some techniques for writing effective argumentation essay.

On education, the great Robert Frost wrote:

"Education is the ability to listen to almost anything without losing your temper or your self-confidence."

Writer Robert Frost

Writing Argumentation Essays

Here are some important techniques to consider when writing argumentation essays.

 Consider Your Audience

It is imperative to identify for whom we are writing. If we are college students, our instructors are our audience, of course. However, we should not assume, because our audience is our instructors and they gave us the assignment, that we do not need to clarify what we are saying. We need not assume that our instructors know, since they are instructors, what we are trying to convey.

As a teacher, I noticed that whenever I pointed out lack of clarity on some of my students' essay papers, some students would tell me that they thought I would know what they meant. The worst thing writers can do is assuming that readers know what the writers are thinking. It is always wise to assume that the audience does not have any idea or background information about what our content.

In addition, considering the audience also means thinking about the level of language we are using. In our case here, since we are writing academically, we must be able to use academic language. If we write for the workplace, we must know for whom and what level of language we ought to use.

 Recognize the Opposing Views

It is always a preferable practice to start the introductory paragraph with a sentence or two introducing the topic and stating the opposing views. In doing so, we are telling readers that we have done our homework. We understand the opposing views and why some hold to them, but we still disagree with those views.

CONSIDER THE FOLLOWING

State Your Main Point in a Convincing Thesis Statement

As with any essay, we need to write a strong introductory paragraph for an argumentation essay. An introductory paragraph should start with a few sentences introducing the topic about which we are writing. The thesis statement should follow these sentences. The thesis statement is, basically, the opinion. It is the point about which we argue.

For example, "Breed-specific legislation is not the answer to preventing dog bites, because it does not make communities safer, it does not address the root of the problem, and it is not fair to responsible owners and good pets." This represents your viewpoint, which you will argue and prove valid throughout the essay.

Develop and Support Your Argument in the Body of the Essay

The body of the essay consists of three supporting paragraphs, with one paragraph devoted to each point of the thesis statement. Of course, each paragraph must start with a strong topic sentence. Then goes on to support it with evidence, such as facts, statistics, examples, anecdotes, and quotes from expert opinions we have researched and will cite properly.

Please note that although a topic sentence may appear at the beginning, middle, or end of a paragraph, or it may even be implied, it is better that we start our paragraph with the topic sentence. Writing the topic sentence at the start of the paragraph will always provide both the writer and the reader with direction and will keep thoughts focused.

CONSIDER THE FOLLOWING

Circumvent Common Errors in Rationalizing

We need to be sure that the premises are logical and that the conclusions correctly follow these premises. It may help to read the essay from an opponent's standpoint. If we held the opposite position of the one we presented in the essay, how convincing the argument is, how valid the premises are, and if there are any fallacies.

If we find weak areas, we take this as an opportunity to think more deeply about the issue chosen and strengthen the support for the position. One can often learn a lot about a topic, and about oneself, when one writes an argumentation essay.

Use Transitional Words and Phrases to Connect Ideas

As you know, in order to keep an essay coherent, we need to use transitional words or phrases between paragraphs as well as between ideas within a paragraph. Transitional words and phrases logically connect sentences and ideas. They provide the reader with directions for how to make sense of the ideas and how these ideas fit together.

In short, transitions help readers follow the process of thinking.

Transitions can vary depending on the type of essay. When we write argumentation essays, we are making connections that build arguments. Transitional words and phrases are also necessary to signal the conclusion of the essay. No matter what type of essay or what essay style, a solid conclusion is very important. Therefore, the way we transition into a conclusion is just as important. In an argumentation essay, this transition can be very valuable.

CONSIDER THE FOLLOWING 193

Below are some transitions that can be used as we move through any element of an argumentation essay.

Transitions	
For the Body	**For the Conclusion**
• First	Finally
• Second	In a word
• Third	In conclusion
• Next	In summary
• Another	In the end
• In addition	Overall
• Moreover	Thus

The Conclusion

The conclusion of an argumentation essay can be very powerful. We use conclusions not only to wrap up all ideas and restate the thesis statement, but also to write an afterthought to enhance the effectiveness of the essay. An afterthought is an idea, response, or explanation that occurs to someone after the writing has been completed.

CONSIDER THE FOLLOWING

Writer T.S. Eliot wrote:

"It is a test (a positive test, I do not assert that it is always valid negatively), that genuine poetry [or writing] can communicate before it is understood."

Writer T.S. Eliot

Chapter Ten: The Non-Native Speaker

A Thought for ESL/EFL Learners

As a non-native speaker of English, I believe that understanding the rules of a language makes acquiring it much easier. In recent years, many ESL teachers and administrators have stopped teaching language rules. They believe that learners acquire a language faster and more efficiently if they are not burdened by the rules. I politely disagree. I believe that if one knows the rules and the reasons for them, one will learn faster and better.

Learning some rules can be helpful. The following are some additional rules that learners may find useful:

- Usually, use a gerund after a preposition.
- The letter *"I"* always comes before *"e"*, except after *"c."* (Believe or Re*cei*ve)
- Learning prefixes and suffixes will help you figure out the meaning of unfamiliar words.
- The verb *to be* is used as an auxiliary verb only in two ways: to make the progressive tense (*We are working*) and to make the passive voice (*The bank was robbed*).
- Remember that the use of prepositions is strictly cultural. There is no explanation as to why in English we use different prepositions than in French, Spanish, Italian, or any other language.

Learning the rules above will make writing a lot easier and a lot more fun.

CONSIDER THE FOLLOWING

Overview of Other Parts of Speech

Words are writer's tools. The more a learner is proficient at word usage, the more accomplished and effective a writer she or he will be. Learners of any foreign language ought to begin by learning the language's parts of speech.

Nouns and Pronouns
A noun names a person, a place, a thing, or an idea. It is also usually the subject of a sentence, as well as an object. For example, look at the following simple sentence:

The girl sat on the chair. The nouns are *girl* and *chair*. In addition, *girl* is the subject (she does the action of the verb *sat*), and *chair* is the object (it is what she takes action on).

Closely related to nouns are pronouns. These are words used in place of one or more nouns and can be singular or plural, just like nouns. Some common pronouns include the following:

- He, him
- She, her
- It
- They, them, their, theirs
- We, us, our, ours
- You, your, yours
- Who, whom, whose
- This, that, which, these, those
- One, another, any, each, either, every

Repeating a noun over and over again can annoy readers, so pronouns are excellent tools for helping us trim repetition. Let me give you two examples. First, here is a sentence in which the noun is repeated:

Leila sat on the chair, and when Leila grew tired,
Leila curled up on Leila's bed for a nap.

Now, see how much better this sounds using pronouns:

Leila sat on the chair, and when she grew tired, she curled up on her bed for a nap.

Adjectives and Adverbs

Adjectives and adverbs modify other words. This means that they make the meaning of the other words more specific by adding descriptive details. Adjectives and adverbs have unique functions, so let us look at each of them.

Adjectives modify, or describe, nouns and pronouns. Here is an example of adjectives modifying nouns:

The pretty child sat on the softest chair.

Can you spot the adjectives? If you chose *pretty* and *softest*, you would be correct. The word *pretty* describes the child, and the word *softest* describes the chair.

Now, here is an example of an adjective modifying a pronoun:

Choosing between all the chairs in the room, the pretty child sat on the softest one.

Do you see how the pronoun *one* takes the place of the noun *chair*? So *softest* modifies the pronoun *one*.

Adverbs, on the other hand, modify verbs. Remember, adjectives modify nouns, and adverbs modify verbs. It is actually easy to remember, since the word *adverb* has the word *verb* in it. Let us look at an example:

 ✢ *The child sat quietly on the chair.*

Do you see the adverb? That is right, it is *quietly*, which describes how the action of the verb *sat* is done. Here is a tip: Adverbs often end in *-LY*, so that is one way you can spot them.

Now, adverbs also do more than describe verbs. They can modify adjectives and other adverbs. They are quite versatile! Here is an example of an adverb modifying an adjective:

 ✢ *The stunningly pretty child sat on the chair.*

The adverb is *stunningly*, and it describes the adjective *pretty*.

Now, here is an example of an adverb modifying another adverb:

 ✢ *The child sat very quietly on the chair.*

The adverb *very* is describing the other adverb *quietly*.

Prepositions

Prepositions show how nouns and pronouns relate to other words in a sentence. They also show "time," depending on the sentence. Like the word *adverb*, the word *preposition* has a built-in clue for how it is used: It has the word *position* inside of it. Here are some examples:

 ✢ *The child sat on the chair.*
 ✢ *We ate dinner before dessert.*

In the first sentence, *on* is the preposition, and it tells us where (the place) the child sat. In the second sentence, *before* is the preposition, and it tells us when (the time) we ate dinner in relation to eating dessert. If we use our clue *position*, we will see that these pre*position*s show us the position of the child in relation to the chair, and the position of dinner in relation to dessert.

Notice also that nouns followed both of these prepositions: (*The chair* and *dessert*). This is one of the few rules in English grammar that will never have an exception. If you use a preposition, you *must* follow it with a noun. Here are some common prepositions:

About, Above, Across, At, Below, Down, From, In, Of, Off, Out, Under.

CONSIDER THE FOLLOWING

Conjunctions:

Conjunctions join other words, phrases, and clauses. The word *conjunction* has a clue inside of it, too: *junction*, which refers to joining. All these built-in clues are certainly handy! Conjunctions come in two groups: *coordinating* and *subordinating*. Let us look at each category.

Coordinating conjunctions join equivalent words, phrases, clauses, and complete sentences. You are probably most familiar with these types of conjunctions, because they are common words like *and*, *but*, *or*, *nor*, *yet*, *for*, and *so*. Here are some examples:

- The boy loved to throw *and* catch the ball.
- The boy threw the ball to his father, *so* his father caught it.
- The father threw the ball back, *but* it went over the neighbor's fence.
- The boy went to play with his friends, *for* they could throw better than his father.

Subordinating conjunctions join two related clauses to each other so that one carries the main idea and one is dependent on the other. In other words, one clause is *subordinate* to the other. The subordinate, or dependent, clause (which starts with the subordinating conjunction) is also no longer a complete sentence. Subordinating conjunctions include the following:

CONSIDER THE FOLLOWING

- After
- Although
- As
- As if
- Because
- Before
- Even if
- Even though
- If
- If only
- Rather than
- Since
- That
- Though
- Unless
- Until
- When
- Where
- Whereas
- Wherever
- Whether
- Which
- While

Here are some examples:

Since the boy left to play with his friends, his father decided to watch baseball on television instead.

The boy came home and watched baseball with his father *because* his friends did not want to play catch.

Subordinating conjunctions also express time, cause and effect, or opposition.

CONSIDER THE FOLLOWING

Punctuation: Commas

We have all had trouble using punctuation at one time or another. Some punctuation rules are clear-cut and indisputable. Others, especially concerning the use of commas, are sometimes debatable. All of the punctuation rules and errors are far too many to list in one lesson—or even in one course, for that matter. So, that is why I have prepared this list of the most common errors I have found in my students' writing.

Let us start with commas. Commas may look harmless, but they can be very powerful—and powerfully confusing! What are they used for?

Commas provide the smallest break in a sentence. The next strongest break comes with the semicolon, and the strongest comes with the period.

Commas have many purposes. They signal that it is time to pause in a sentence. They separate clauses to clarify meaning. They link items together in a series. They show what is not essential, but still interesting, in a sentence. And they introduce quotations. Commas are extremely versatile punctuation marks; so let us see how to use them skillfully.

CONSIDER THE FOLLOWING

In Compound Sentences

A compound sentence has two or more independent clauses joined by either a comma and a conjunction or just a semicolon (;). (An independent clause, remember, is a word group that has a subject and a verb and that can stand alone as a sentence.) The usual conjunctions are the coordinating conjunctions, which we are already familiar with (*and, or, but, nor, yet, so, for*).

Here are two formulas you can use to remember the rules about punctuating compound sentences:

With a comma: Independent clause + , + coordinating conjunction + independent clause.

With a semicolon: Independent clause + ; + independent clause.

Let us look at two examples of these rules:

> With a comma: She feels ill, but she is going to school.

With a semicolon: Toni wants to visit his grandparents in Spain this summer; on his budget, though, he can only afford dinner and a movie.

Students sometimes do not join independent clauses correctly and make one of two errors: either a run-on sentence or a comma splice. We will look at each one so that you can safely avoid it in your writing.

First, if we forget to use a punctuation mark and a coordinating conjunction between independent clauses, we create a *run-on sentence*:

Learning how to write effectively is useful for everyone it is essential for college students.

Did you get confused as you read this sentence? I did, and I wrote it! That is the effect run-on sentences have. They are called *run-on sentences* because the two independent clauses run together and the sentence goes on and on. Punctuation will make it much clearer, but it must be the correct punctuation in order to work.

For example, if we use a comma without a coordinating conjunction, we will have created another error: a *comma splice*. Here is what this looks like:

Learning how to write effectively is useful for everyone; it is essential for college students.

To correct the comma splice in this sentence, you have the following four choices.

1. Use a comma and a coordinating conjunction:

Learning how to write effectively is useful for everyone, but it is essential for college students.

2. Use only a semicolon, or use a semicolon with a conjunction:

3. Learning how to write effectively is useful for everyone; it is essential for college students.

Learning how to write effectively is useful for everyone; but it is essential for college students.

4. Separate the two independent clauses into separate sentences:

Learning how to write effectively is useful for everyone. It is essential for college students.

CONSIDER THE FOLLOWING

5. Restructure the sentence, perhaps by subordinating one of the clauses:

While it is useful for everyone to learn how to write effectively, it is essential for college students.

With Introductory Phrases and Clauses

We also need to use a comma after an introductory phrase or clause. Here is an example of a phrase:

With such knowledge behind her, the applicant felt more confident during her interview.

Here is an example of a clause:

Because she had so much knowledge behind her, the applicant felt more comfortable during her interview.

What happens if we leave out the comma? Here is an example:

Before eating the boys washed their hands.

Were you wondering at first who did something before eating the boys? Without a comma after *eating*, it sounds like a horrible monster came along and ate the boys! What a difference the comma makes:

Before eating, the boys washed their hands.
Now there are no monsters—just boys with clean hands.

CONSIDER THE FOLLOWING

In Series or Lists

As I was learning English, I found that I was repeatedly failing to add commas between items in a series. So, I hope the information below will help you avoid the errors I used to make.

The rule about items in a series is very simple and clear—one of the few rules that is clear!

When you write a series that has three or more items, you should separate each item with a comma. Remember that items in a series may be single words, phrases, or even clauses.

Here are some examples:

Single words:

My favorite vegetables are carrots, broccoli, and squash.
Phrases: Causes of cancer may include smoking cigarettes, eating unhealthy foods, being exposed to harmful chemicals, and sunbathing for long periods of time. Clauses: Juliette fixed dinner, Antoine prepared dessert, and Valerie put flowers on the table.

Here is a special tip: When the items in a series are made of phrases, do not accidentally put a comma in the middle of the phrase. For instance, in the second example above, if I had put a comma between the words *smoking* and *cigarettes*, I would have changed the meaning of this item. So, always make sure you know what makes up the series or list: single words, phrases, or clauses.

Teachers and writers debate whether to use a comma before the last item, where there is an "*and*". However, I prefer using that last comma because it prevents ambiguity and misreading.

Now, here is a good question. How do you separate several separate lists in the same sentence? When you have a series of lists in which the items are already separated by commas, you need to separate each series with a semicolon. This may sound confusing, but once you see it, you will understand. So, here is an example:

Jennifer's many chores included cooking, baking, and serving dinner; washing, ironing, and folding the laundry; and weeding, mowing, and edging the lawn.

Do you see the three sets of series? Each contains three verbs that apply to one object (*the lawn, dinner*, and *the laundry*). Sentences with a series of lists are often very long and confusing, but the punctuation is the key to making them clear.

With Restrictive and Nonrestrictive Modifiers

You probably remember this, but just to refresh your memory, I will remind you of what a modifier is. Simply, it is a word or phrase that describes (modifies) another word or phrase.

Sometimes, modifiers are essential to the meaning of the nouns they describe. These are called *restrictive*, because they restrict the meaning of the noun to something specific. Do not use commas to set restrictive modifiers apart from the nouns they describe. The commas will signal that the modifier could be taken out and not change the meaning of the sentence. However, this would not be true; the meaning would change.

Here are some examples of restrictive modifiers:
The teacher who comes from Egypt teaches writing.
The student who scores the highest points will receive an award.
In the first sentence, the modifier *who comes from Egypt* identifies which teacher gives instruction about writing. If we mistakenly set apart this modifier with commas, the sentence would say: *The teacher teaches writing.* That does not tell us enough information, does it? Which teacher are we referring to?

In the second sentence, the modifier *who scores the highest points* specifies which student will receive an award: only the student with the highest points. Does this make sense?

At other times, modifiers are not essential to the meaning of the nouns they describe. In this case, they are called *nonrestrictive*, or sometimes *nonessential*. The modifier provides interesting information, but if you removed it, the meaning of the noun and the sentence would stay the same. You must set off nonrestrictive clauses with a pair of commas, one before the clause and one after it. Here are some examples for you to consider:

> Professor Bebawi, who is from Egypt, teaches writing.
> Joan, who scored the highest points, will receive an award.

In these two sentences, Professor Bebawi and Joan are identified by their proper names. Their names make the meaning of the nouns specific, so we know exactly who teaches writing and who will receive an award.

So, the information between the pair of commas is nonrestrictive—it adds interesting detail, but it is not essential to the meaning of the sentence.

Please understand that nonrestrictive clauses are not examples of wordiness and therefore bad writing.

The terms *essential* and *nonessential* do not mean *good* and *bad* in this context. They just tell us which clause does not need commas and which clause does need commas.

Punctuation: Semicolons, Colons, and Periods

How are you doing so far? I am very sure that you remember most of this information, but maybe you do not use it every day. When you do not use a rule or technique often, you can sometimes have difficulty remembering it. I hope that you are finding this information helpful and are ready to continue. Let us move forward with a look at more punctuation.

Semicolons, Colons, and Dashes

Since we have already used the semicolon a few times in the previous chapter, we will start with this punctuation mark. Semicolons are stronger than commas but weaker than periods. Where a period will separate any two independent clauses, a semicolon will separate only two independent clauses that relate very closely to each other. The clauses that a semicolon separates must continue one idea.

Here are a few semicolon rules to remember:

> Use a semicolon between independent clauses not connected by a coordinating conjunction.
> Mahatma Gandhi was a champion of civil rights and the method of nonviolence; Martin Luther King Jr. was greatly influenced by his example.
>
> Use a semicolon to separate independent clauses that are long or complex.

Bridget tried to make her flight reservations, but the airline's computer system was down; so she has decided to wait until tomorrow before trying again, hoping that the discount ticket price will still be in effect.

Use a semicolon in a series of lists that already have commas between the items.

Spring gives us the joy of greening trees, blossoming flowers, and singing birds; summer relaxes us with bright blue skies, sunny days, and family vacations; and autumn invigorates us with bracing winds, dazzlingly colored trees, and fragrant fireplaces.

Is all of this clear to you? If so, let us move on to a punctuation mark that many people confuse with semicolons: colons.

What jobs do colons do? They introduce lists, quotations, and instructions, and they also provide bridges to explanations. Basically, they direct our attention to the material that follows them.

They provide a stronger, more definite stop than a semicolon, and semicolons can never be used in the same ways that colons can.

Here are a few examples of colons at work:

With a list: Cigarette smoke causes problems for three types of people: those with allergies, those with asthma, and those with heart problems.

With a quotation: President John F. Kennedy, in his famous inaugural speech, challenged us with these words: "Ask not what your country can do for you; ask what you can do for your country." With instructions: To make a glass of ice water, perform the following steps: Pour cold water into a glass. Put two or three ice cubes into the glass of water.

With an explanation: The dog gave up hope of going for a walk: Her owner sat transfixed in front of the TV set, and no amount of barking at her would get her attention.

One tip to remember about colons is to not use them after verbs. For example, do not punctuate the following sentence like this: *My favorite opera singers are: Enrico Caruso, Pavarotti, and Placido Domingo.* The colon that comes after *"are"* is not necessary and, worse, is an error.

Like the colon, the dash also introduces explanations, but in a less formal way. Dashes have a quick, vigorous sense of movement and can grab the readers' attention right away. They are very useful in strongly emphasizing thoughts. In addition, they also set off nonrestrictive clauses with more power than commas. Let us see some dashes in action: With explanations: Friedrich warned Marcel not to play tangos on the accordion—when he hears the music, Friedrich cannot help but dance.

For emphasis: It was just what the doctor feared—acute appendicitis.

With nonrestrictive clauses: The Hansen's' trip to Sweden—a lifelong dream come true—was a glorious time of long bike rides through forests and alongside pristine lakes.

Dashes have become so useful that they risk being overused. So be careful that you do not rely on them too much. Instead, be discerning as you choose your punctuation marks, Periods, Question Marks, and Exclamation Points.

Periods, question marks, and exclamation points are all types of concluding punctuation because they end sentences. In English, a sentence will only need one mark of punctuation at the end, unlike some other languages that begin and end sentences with question marks or exclamation points.

These marks are very straightforward, so we will move through them quickly.

- Use a period at the end of a statement or a command:

The hungry bears foraged for huckleberries.
Stop making that noise.
In the United States, a period (and also a comma) goes inside concluding quotation marks:

Tyrone said, "In the summer, I like to go swimming in the lake."

- Use a question mark at the end of a question:

What time does our plane leave?

In the United States, a question mark goes inside a quotation *only if* the quotation itself is a question. If a sentence is a question but ends with a quotation that is not a question, then the question mark goes outside the quotation. Here is how this looks:

Lama wondered, "Why does John always leave me to do all the cooking?"

Why was Lama angry when John said, "Since you are busy, I am going golfing by myself"?

- Use an exclamation point to emphasize a thought, to give a command, to show anger or disgust, to show surprise, or to highlight humor. Do not overuse this punctuation mark, however; it will draw too much attention to itself and become annoying. One witty writer said, "The exclamation point is like the horn on your car—use it only when you have to" (Patricia T. O'Conner, *Woe Is I*). Here are some examples of this loud punctuation mark:

 *Do not overuse exclamation points!*

I will not tolerate such rudeness!
What is this—a birthday cake for me!
He thought Donald Trump had nice hair!

In the United States, exclamation points follow the same rules as question marks when it comes to quotations:

Henri shouted to us, "Bon voyage!"
With the rent due next week, Simone was astounded when Julio casually told her, *"I quit my job"!*

As you have seen, punctuation is very important when you write in English. It guides your readers along the path of your thoughts and helps them understand what you have to say more clearly. It also helps set the pace of your writing. Think of punctuation marks as road signs—they tell readers when to stop, when to slow down, and when something is coming.

ESL/EFL Problem Spots

Here are the most common problems the ESL/EFL learner faces while acquiring the new language.

The use of helping verbs with main verbs:

Helping verbs, such as modals and do, are followed by main verbs in the simple form without conjugation. It does not matter if the subject is plural, singular or third person.

For example: *I will go to England.*

> You will go to England.
> She will go to England

Notice that we did not conjugate the main verb (go).
We did not say, for instance, "She will goes to England."

Another example: *Do you speak English?*

> Does she speak English?
> Did he speak English in his country?

Notice that we did not conjugate the main verb (speak).
We did not say, for instance, "*Does she speaks English?*"

Also, notice that we did not use (to) in front of the main verb. We cannot say, "*Does she to speak English?*" or " *She will to go to England.*"

In other situations, we conjugate the main verb after helping verbs to indicate a particular tense or form. For example, the formula for the perfect tense:

Have + Verb in the past participle = I have eaten dinner already.

Notice that the main verb (eat) is in the past participle form, (eaten).

The passive voice formula:

Be + Verb in the past participle = the letter was written by my sister.

Notice that the main verb (write) is in the past participle form (written).

The progressive formula:

Be + Verb in the –ing form = She is learning English.
Notice that the main verb (learn) is in the present participle form – ing (learning).
So, be cautious when using helping verbs.

The Conditional Sentences:

In conditional sentences, choose verbs with care. A conditional sentence is one that shows something depending on something else. Sometimes such sentences can confuse the ESL/EFL learner.

Real Condition:

In real condition sentences when the action happens repeatedly, use present tense.

For example: Whenever it rains, she stays home.

In real condition sentences, when the result will most likely occur, use future.

For example: *If you study, you will succeed.*

Unreal Condition:

In unreal condition sentences, both the condition and the result are not likely to occur. The verb in the dependent clause should be in the unreal form (the past tense) and the verb in the independent clause should be preceded by would, could or might.

For example: ***If I had money, I would buy a BMW.***

Notice that I used verb have in the past form because it is unreal. I really do not have money, but "if I had," I would buy a MBW.

Unreal conditional sentences can be about events that did not happen. In such case, we use past perfect in the "if" clause to indicate that the action was unreal in the past. The verb in the independent clause consists of would have, could have, or might have plus the past participle. This form is called "Modal Perfect."

For example: ***If I had saved enough money, I would have traveled***

Notice that I used the past perfect in the "if" clause to indicate that the action, (save money), is unreal because I did not save money. The independent clause consists of the modal perfect (would have traveled) to also indicate that the action (travel) is unreal.

Unreal conditional is also used in conditions contrary to fact to speculate about situations that are unreal. In this case we use the unreal form of verb (be) in the dependent clause, and we use would, could, or might plus the main verb in its base form.

Remember: The unreal form of verb (be) is always (were). It doe not matter whether the subject is plural, or singular, the verb will always be (were).

For example: *If I were rich, I would help the poor.*

Here I am stating that I am not rich, but in the unreal situation of being rich (if I were rich), the result would be helping the poor (I would help the poor).

CONSIDER THE FOLLOWING

Gerunds and Infinitives

This is a trouble spot for the ESL/EFL learner. We are often wondering whether we should use a gerund or an infinitive. To understand how this works, we must know what is a gerund. A gerund is the –ing form of a verb, such as working, sleeping, studying. In this form, it is not a verb at all; it is a noun. Therefore, we need to remember that a gerund is a noun. We can replace a noun with the pronoun (it).

Read this sentence: *Reading enhances our ability to write.*

Now ask yourself what the verb of this sentence is. Your answer will obviously be (enhances). In this case, "reading" is the subject of the sentences; it is a noun. I can replace "reading" with the pronoun "it" and the sentence will still be correct.

It enhances our ability to write.

On the other hand, an infinitive is the verb preceded by "to" meaning, "to do something." It is not a noun; it is an action. In the sentence above, "our ability to write" means our ability to do it.

This distinction has always worked for me. So, when you are in doubt as to whether to use a gerund or an infinitive, ask yourself if it is "it" or "to do it." If you can use "it," a gerund will be correct. If you must use "to do it," an infinitive should be your choice.

Let us try it. Complete the following sentence using "write"

I enjoy ------.

To choose the right form, ask yourself whether you can say, "I enjoy (it)" or "I enjoy (to do) it."

The response will be, "*I enjoy 'it'*.

Therefore, the sentence should be, "*I enjoy writing.*"

Here is a list of verbs that are followed by gerunds:

>Admit – appreciate – avoid – deny – enjoy – finish
>Miss – postpone – practice – quit – recall – resist

Here is a list of verbs that are followed by infinitives:

>Agree – ask – claim – decide – expect – have –
>Hope – manage – offer – plan – pretend – promise –
>Refuse – wait – want – wish

Here are verbs that can be followed by either an infinitive or a gerund:

Begin – continue – hate – like – love – start
Try using these verbs to get a sense of how they function. You need a lot of practice.

The Use of Articles "A" "An" and "The"
There are many nouns in English that cannot be counted. We need to know such nouns so we may use the proper verb form that agrees with the noun.

For the nouns that we can count, we use the articles "a" or "an" before the singular count noun. For example, "I have an apple;" and "I have a pen."

Notice that we used "an" with the noun "apple" because apple starts with a vowel. We used "a" with the noun "pen" because pen starts with a consonant. So, always use "an" with nouns that begin with a vowel and use "a" with nouns that begin with a consonant.

CONSIDER THE FOLLOWING 220

Using "The"

Note that we use the article "the" with most nouns whose specific identity is known. Usually the identity will be clear for one of the following reasons:

(1) The noun has been previously mentioned.
(2) Using superlatives such as 'best' and 'most makes noun's identity specific.
(3) The noun's identity is clear because of the context.

We should not use the article "the" with:

(1) Proper nouns such as names of people.
(2) Plural nouns that indicate the meaning 'all' or 'in general'.

    For example: In Egypt, rice is preferred to other grains. Notice that we did not say "the rice."

Other Problem Areas for the ESL/EFL Learner

(1)   Omitting the subject of an independent clause.

Sometimes a learner may omit the subject of an independent clause. For example, one may say: *"Your sister is very beautiful; seems intelligent, too."*

Notice that the subject in the second clause is not present. Therefore, we need to correct it to read:

"Your sister is very beautiful; she seems intelligent, too."

(2)   Repeating the subject of a sentence.

Non-native speakers tend to repeat the subject in a sentence. For example, one may incorrectly say: "My brother he is in Mexico." We do not need the pronoun "he" in that sentence.

(3)   Confusing the participial adjectives: Present Participles and Past participles.

Both present and past participles may be used as adjectives. One way you can figure out which to use is deciding who the doer and the receiver are. If the noun you want to describe is the cause of the action, use a present participle (-ing). If the "receiver," the noun that receives the action, is the noun that you want to describe, use the past participle.

For example: *"The movie was depressing. I was depressed."*

CONSIDER THE FOLLOWING 222

Here the cause of the action is the movie and the receiver is I. Another example: "*The class is boring; the students are bored.*"

The class is the cause and the students are the receivers.

According to the Bedford Handbook for Writers, the participles that cause the most trouble for nonnative speakers are those describing mental state:

Annoying / annoyed

Boring / bored
Confusing / confused
Depressing / depressed
Exciting / excited
Exhausting / exhausted
Fascinating / fascinated
Frightening / frightened
Satisfying / satisfied

When you come across these words, always do the test. Ask yourself who the doer or the cause of the action is and who the receiver is. Use the present participle (–ing) form to describe the doer and use the past participle (–en) form to describe the receiver.

(4)   Confusing prepositions of time and place.

Prepositions that show time and place can be confusing to the ESL/EFL learner. One of the reasons why these prepositions are difficult is that the difference between them is merely idiomatic.

CONSIDER THE FOLLOWING

Here is a possible aid for you to decide which preposition to use:

TIME:
>At: for a specific time. "*I get up at 7:00.*"
>On: on a specific day. "*I was born on a Friday.*"
>In: in a part of time. "*I drink tea in the afternoon.*"

PLACE:
>At: at a location. "*Maria is at home.*"
>
>On: on the surface of something. "*She put the glass on the table.*"

Conclusion:

Much of the materials covered here can easily be learned through interaction. Learning a new language can sometimes involve learning about the culture where the target language is spoken. Listening to people talk, reading, watching movies and of course asking questions can enhance your skills and speed up your learning process. I encourage you to actively engage yourselves in the learning process. Listen, observe, and learn.

CONSIDER THE FOLLOWING 225

Application and Review

Can you take what you have learned about essay writing and use it in other settings, such as the workplace? The answer is yes! Here are some tips:

Applying What You Have Learned to the Workplace
In real-life situations, most of us will have to write e-mail, a memo, a letter, or a report. Writing these documents is not much different from writing an essay. The same rules and techniques apply. However, there is a major difference between college writing and workplace writing.

The goal of college writing is to improve your learning and critical thinking. When you are writing for college, you are demonstrating your knowledge of a topic. Your essays will be longer and sometimes involve research. In contrast, **workplace writing is more specific**. It conveys information and procedures in very practical terms. This type of writing, though, does not require fewer skills on the part of the writer.

Whatever your reason for writing, you need to know your audience. It is important that when writing for the workplace, you use gender-neutral vocabulary to equally include and show respect for all the people you work with.

Also, in the workplace, you may need to use the passive voice more often. Let me explain this a little further. In the workplace, you may find it necessary to use the passive voice either to emphasize the receiver of the action or to hide the doer of the action.

We see examples of this in advertisements all the time. A writer might say, "It has been shown that our product is the most effective in the market." The passive voice is used here intentionally to avoid stating who the doer was—who showed that the product was the most effective.

At any rate, regardless of the reason for writing, we will want to observe all the rules we have examined in this course. By doing this, we will ensure that our final drafts are clear and effective. So, let us review some of the key points we have learned about the writing and editing processes.

CONSIDER THE FOLLOWING

Key Points About the Writing Process

Let us start with topic sentences. You learned that a topic sentence tells the reader what each paragraph is about. To be most effective, it is wise to make your topic sentence the first sentence in a paragraph. Each topic sentence you write should have the following characteristics:

- It should set up one controlling idea for the paragraph.
- It should be a complete sentence.
- It should not be an announcement of what you are going to say; it should directly state your idea.
- It should not be too broad or too narrow.
- It should not be vague.

Next, let us review what we know about thesis statements. A thesis statement tells us what an entire essay will be about; it will communicate several key ideas. The difference between a topic sentence and a thesis statement is this: A topic sentence gives us the controlling idea of each paragraph, while a thesis statement gives us the controlling thoughts of a whole essay. A thesis statement gives us the big picture, and topic sentences give focus to the details.

With the exception of the single controlling idea, all the characteristics that apply to good topic sentences will also apply to good thesis statements.

Key Points About the Editing Process

Now, let us remind ourselves of some of the key editing issues we need to look out for as we polish our writing.

1. **Word Choice**:

   Choose your words carefully when you write. Select words that are precise and appropriate for your purpose. Eliminate slang, clichés, and pretentious and vague words. Also, if you can say something with one word instead of many, use the one word.

2. **Transitions**:

   Transitions are crucial for the unity and cohesiveness of your writing. They help readers follow and understand your thoughts. Be sure that you choose the right transitional words based on the particular needs of your essay. For instance, if you are writing a compare and contrast essay, you should use transitions that demonstrate similarities (*likewise, similarly*) and differences (*in contrast, however*).

3. **Subject-Verb Agreement**:

   Check every subject and verb to make sure they match in number. If the subject is singular, then the verb needs to be singular. If the subject is plural, the verb needs to be plural. Compound subjects joined by *and* take plural verbs. However, with compound subjects joined by *or*, the noun closest to the verb will determine whether the verb should be singular or plural.

4. **Verb Tenses**:

Keep your verb tenses consistent throughout your sentences and paragraphs. Also, use the correct form of the verb (its inflection) to express the tense you want (present, past, or future).

5. **Modifiers**:

Make sure your modifiers are clear, are placed as close as possible to the nouns they describe, and do not dangle. When your sentence begins with a modifier that is a participial phrase (an-*ing* verb phrase without a stated subject), the subject needs to come directly after it to prevent confusion (and unintended laughter!).

6. **Proper Punctuation**:

Watch out especially for run-on sentences and comma splices. Also, be sure to include commas in series so the words do not run together and cause confusion. Note what is essential and nonessential information. Use commas after introductory clauses to prevent misreading. When you are unsure about which punctuation mark to use, look it up in your grammar book. This book will be very helpful to you; even today I continue to use mine!

7. **Spelling**:

Do not depend on your computer's spell-check feature to make sure your writing is accurate. It will often miss homophones and homonyms, for example. Also, sometimes this feature might select a completely different word from what you meant. So, get in the habit of using your dictionary, whether it is online or a book, to check any word you doubt.

As a final note, many of my students ask how long a good sentence should be. While this is a difficult question to answer, many teachers advise that a sentence should have an average length of 22 words. If you find that some of your sentences are too long, break them into shorter ones. Of course, a good writer will vary the length of sentences in each paragraph.

I have greatly enjoyed writing this book. I hope, now that you have completed the course, you currently feel more confident about writing than when you started reading this text. It is important that you keep writing; it is like learning a musical instrument—practice, practice, and practice.

CONSIDER THE FOLLOWING

The great writer Leo Tolstoy once wrote about art and writing is an art:

"Art is not a handicraft, it is the transmission of feeling the artist has experienced."

The Infamous Tolstoy

CONGRATULATIONS

Sabri g. Bebawi

I wish to thank all my students and those who have given me permission to use their writings.

I also wish to emphasize that the authors' photos in this book, to the best-researched educated knowledge of the writer, are in Public Domain and free of royalty.

www.ingramcontent.com/pod-product-compliance
Lightning Source LLC
Chambersburg PA
CBHW041431300426
44115CB00001B/2